TRUE COLORS

An EFL Course for Real Communication

2

Jay Maurer
Irene E. Schoenberg

Joan Saslow
Series Director

Longman

True Colors: An EFL Course for Real Communication 2

Pearson Education, 10 Bank Street, White Plains, NY 10606

Senior acquisitions editor: Allen Ascher
Director of design and production: Rhea Banker
Managing editor: Halley Gatenby
Production editor: Christine Cervoni
Cover design: Rhea Banker
Text design: Word & Image Design
Text composition: Word & Image Design
Illustrations: Pierre Berthiaume, Jocelyn Bouchard, Kasia Charko, Eric Colquhoun,
    Quack Communications, Brian Hughes, Paul McCusker, Carole Peloquin,
    Dusan Petricic, Stephen Quinlan, Richard Row, Philip Scheuer, Steve Shulman,
    Teco, Margot Thompson, Angela Vaculik
Photography: Gilbert Duclos

Library of Congress Cataloging-in-Publication Data

Maurer, Jay.
    True colors: an EFL course for real communication/Jay Maurer; Irene E. Schoenberg;
    Joan Saslow, series director
        p. cm.
    ISBN 0-201-87808-9
    1. English language—Textbooks for foreign speakers.
2. Communication. I. Schoenberg, Irene. II. Saslow, Joan M. III. Title.

PE1128.M3548   1998

428.2'4—dc21   97-12071
                                                        CIP

ISBN: 0–201–69515–4

    14 15-CRK-05 04 03

Contents

Scope and Sequence of Specific Content and Skills

UNIT	Social Language	Vocabulary	Grammar	Listening
1 I was thinking of asking Kate out. page 2	How to: • express location • get reacquainted • express greetings • tell a story about the past • make an invitation • accept or decline an invitation	• expressions of location • greetings and responses • social activities • ways to accept an invitation • present and future time expressions	• the past continuous • the past continuous and the simple past tense • the present continuous and *have to* for future actions	Type: • a conversation Comprehension Skill: • focus attention
2 How many will, and how many won't? page 14	How to: • talk about the future • ask for a favor • offer help	• everyday favors we do for others • fruits and vegetables	• *will* as future • *will* and *won't* for willingness and refusal	Types: • a conversation about the future • a conversation about willingness Comprehension Skill: • focus attention
3 It's the softest leather in the world. page 26	How to: • compare people, places, and things • ask for and give clarification • exchange something in a store • state a problem • compare things (more practice)	• clothing sizes • clothing materials • problems with fit	• the comparative form of adjectives • the superlative form of adjectives	Type: • a conversation in a store Comprehension Skill: • focus attention
4 I haven't seen you for days. page 38	How to: • talk about illness • ask about someone's absence • offer sympathy • suggest a course of action • express sympathy	• ailments • questions about health • expressions of sympathy • words that describe how people feel • remedies	• the present perfect—meaning • the present perfect—form	Type: • a conversation about illness Comprehension Skills: • determine context • focus attention
5 What do you think I should do? page 50	How to: • ask for and give advice • suggest an alternative	• personal items • places and things in the house	• *should* • *could*	Type: • a radio editorial Comprehension Skills: • determine context • analysis of point of view
Review of Units 1–5 page 62				
6 Aren't you Dick's brother-in-law? page 74	How to: • make small talk • suggest future actions • confirm identity • name family relationships	• adjectives to describe the weather • family relationships	• negative questions • *why* in negative questions	Type: • a conversation about getting lost Comprehension Skills: • determine context • focus attention
7 We'd better find a gas station—fast! page 86	How to: • describe quantities • request and offer service • warn someone	• words and phrases that tell "how many" and "how much" • at the gas station • on the highway	• quantifiers • *had better*	Types: • a narration • a conversation with police officer Comprehension Skills: • inference and interpretation • understanding meaning from context • focus attention
8 I'd like to make a reservation. page 98	How to: • make a reservation • make a complaint • express preferences	• kinds of hotel rooms • in the hotel room	• the real conditional • *would rather*	Type: • radio advertisements for hotels Comprehension Skill: • focus attention
9 I can't stand filing! page 110	How to: • describe something you like or dislike • greet a friend • promise to talk later	• words that describe what you like and dislike • service occupations • more occupations	• gerunds	Type: • a telephone conversation about likes and dislikes Comprehension Skill: • focus attention
10 We'll have to make a deposit right away. page 122	How to: • talk about future abilities and obligations • ask someone for money • exchange currency	• money and banking • social activities	• *will be able to* • *will have to*	Type: • recorded information on a telephone Comprehension Skills: • determine context • focus attention
Review of Units 6–10 page 134				

Reading	Writing	Pronunciation	Expression of Opinions
Types: • a photo story • a business magazine article Comprehension Skills: • confirming content • understanding meaning from context	Task: • advertisement responses Skill: • concise correspondence	• /ʃ/ and /tʃ/	• differences in what men and women look for in love • advantages and disadvantages of romantic relationships at work
Types: • a photo story • a class discussion transcript Comprehension Skills: • understanding meaning from context • factual recall • interpretation and analysis	Task: • a paragraph Skills: • description • indention	• /v/ and /w/	• necessity of obeying rules and laws
Types: • a photo story • a business letter Comprehension Skills: • confirming content • identifying the main idea • understanding meaning from context	Task: • a business letter Skills: • persuasion • business letter style	• rising intonation to clarify	• qualities of good and bad sales personnel
Types: • a photo story • a magazine article Comprehension Skills: • confirming content • understanding meaning from context • identifying the main idea	Task: • a get-well letter Skill: • informal letter to someone you know	• /n/, /ŋ/, and /m/	• various ways to respond to medical problems and hardships
Types: • a photo story • an interview Comprehension Skills: • understanding meaning from context • interpretation and analysis • confirming content	Task: • a letter to a magazine column Skill: • informal letter to someone you don't know	• /ʊ/ and /u/	• parental pressure versus parental encouragement
Types: • a photo story • a magazine article Comprehension Skills: • confirming content • interpretation and analysis • factual recall	Tasks: • an invitation to a party • a letter of regret that you can't attend Skill: • written directions to a place	• /t/ and /θ/	• gender differences in conversation styles • regional differences in conversation styles
Type: • a magazine article Comprehension Skill: • understanding meaning from context	Task: • an e-mail letter to the editor of a newspaper Skills: • persuasion • e-mail style	• /ð/ and /d/	• driving ability of old people versus young people
Types: • a photo story • a personal letter Comprehension Skills: • understanding meaning from context • drawing conclusions	Tasks: • a thank-you note • addressing an envelope Skills: • expressing thanks for a gift • addressing an envelope	• /dʒ/ and /y/	• problems inherent in traveling
Types: • a photo story • a magazine article and questionnaire Comprehension Skills: • understanding meaning from context • drawing conclusions	Task: • an expository paragraph Skill: • paragraph development	• rising intonation to confirm information	• likes and dislikes about the work environment
Types: • a photo story • a magazine article Comprehension Skills: • understanding meaning from context • drawing conclusions	Task: • a composition Skills: • using a title • composition development	• /v/ and /b/	• attitudes about borrowing and lending money

Acknowledgments

●●●●●●●●●●●●●●●●●●●●●●●●●●●●●●

The authors and series director wish to acknowledge with gratitude the following consultants, reviewers, and piloters—our partners in the development of *True Colors*.

Consultants

Berta de Llano, Puebla, Mexico • **Luis Fernando Gómez J.**, School of Education, University of Antioquia, Colombia • **Irma K. Ghosn**, Lebanese American University, Byblos, Lebanon • **Annie Hu**, Fu-Jen Catholic University, Taipei, Taiwan • **Nancy Lake**, CEL-LEP, São Paulo, Brazil • **Frank Lambert**, Pagoda Foreign Language Institute, Seoul, Korea • **Kazuhiko Yoshida**, Kobe University, Kobe City, Japan.

Reviewers and Piloters

Lucia Adrian, EF Language Schools, Miami, Florida, USA • **Ronald Aviles**, Instituto Chileno Norteamericano, Chuquicamata, Chile • **Liliana Baltra**, Instituto Chileno Norteamericano, Santiago, Chile • **Paulo Roberto Berkelmans**, CEL-LEP, São Paulo, Brazil • **Luis Beze**, Casa Thomas Jefferson, Brasília, Brazil • **Martin T. Bickerstaff,** ELS Language Centers, Oakland, California, USA • **Mary C. Black**, Institute of North American Studies, Barcelona, Spain • **James Boyd**, ECC Foreign Language Institute, Osaka, Japan • **Susan Bryan de Martínez**, Instituto Mexicano Norteamericano, Monterrey, Mexico • **Hugo A. Buitano**, Instituto Chileno Norteamericano, Arica, Chile • **Gary Butzbach**, American Language Center, Rabat, Morocco • **Herlinda Canto**, Universidad Popular Autónoma del Estado de Puebla, Mexico • **Rigoberto Castillo**, Colegio de CAFAM, Santafé de Bogotá, Colombia • **Tina M. Castillio,** Santafé de Bogotá, Colombia • **Amparo Clavijo Olarte**, Universidad Distrital, Santafé de Bogotá, Colombia • **Graciela Conocente**, Asociación Mendocina de Intercambio Cultural Argentino Norteamerica, Argentina • **Greg Conquest**, Yokohama Gaigo Business College, Japan • **Eduardo Corbo**, IETI, Salto, Uruguay • **Marilia Costa**, Instituto Brasil-Estados Unidos, Rio de Janeiro, Brazil • **Miles Craven**, Nihon University, Shizuoka, Japan • **Michael Davidson**, EF Language Schools, Miami, Florida, USA • **Celia de Juan**, UNICO, UAG, Guadalajara, Mexico • **Laura de Marín**, Centro Colombo Americano, Medellín, Colombia • **Montserrat Muntaner Djmal**, Instituto Brasil-Estados Unidos, Rio de Janeiro, Brazil • **Deborah Donnelley de García**, ITESM-Campus Querétaro, Mexico • **Rosa Erlichman**, União Cultural, São Paulo, Brazil • **Patricia Escalante Aruaz,** Universidad de Costa Rica, San Bedro de Montes de Oca, Costa Rica • **Guadalupe Espinoza**, ITESM-Campus Querétaro, Mexico • **Suad Farkouh**, ESL Consultant to Philadelphia National Schools, Amman, Jordan • **Niura R.H. Ferreria**, Centro Cultural Brasil Estados Unidos, Guarapuava, Brazil • **Fernando Fleurquin**, Alianza Cultural Uruguay-EEUU, Montevideo, Uruguay • **Patricia Fleury**, Casa Thomas Jefferson, Brasília, Brazil • **Patricia Foncea**, Colegio Jesualdo, Santiago, Chile • **Areta Ulhana Galat**, Centro Cultural Brasil Estados Unidos, Curitiba, Brazil • **Christina Gitsaki**, Nagoya University of Commerce and Business Administration, Japan • **Julie Harris de Peyré**, Universidad del Valle, Guatemala • **Ruth Hassell de Hernández**, UANL, Mexico • **John Hawkes,** EF International School, Santa Barbara, California, USA • **Rose M. Hernández**, University of Puerto Rico-Bayamón, Puerto Rico • **Susan Hills**, EF International School of English, San Diego, California, USA • **Jan Kelley**, EF International School, Santa Barbara, California, USA • **Mia Kim**, Kyung Hee University, Seoul, Korea • **Junko Kobayashi**, Sankei International College, Tokyo, Japan • **Gil Lancaster**, Academy Istanbul, Istanbul, Turkey • **Mónica Lobo**, Santiago, Chile • **Luz Adriana Lopera**, Centro Colombo Americano, Medellín, Colombia • **Eva Irene Loya**, ITESM-Campus Querétaro, Mexico • **Mary Maloy Lara**, Instituto John F. Kennedy, Tehuacán, Mexico • **Meire de Jesus Marion**, Associação Alumni, São Paulo, Brazil • **Juliet Marlier**, Universidad de las Américas, Puebla, Mexico • **Yolanda Martínez**, Instituto D'Amicis, Puebla, Mexico • **Neil McClelland**, Shimonoseki City University, Japan • **Regina Celia Pereira Mendes**, Instituto Brasil-Estados Unidos, Rio de Janeiro, Brazil • **Jim Miller**, Yokohama Gaigo Business College, Japan • **Fiona Montarry,** The American Language Center, Casablanca, Morocco • **Luiz Claudio Monteiro**, Casa Thomas Jefferson, Brasília, Brazil • **Angelita Oliveira Moreno**, ICBEU, Belo Horizonte, Brazil • **Ahmed Mohammad Motala,** King Fahd University of Petroleum & Minerals, Dhahran, Saudi Arabia • **William Richard Munzer**, Universidad IDEAS de Bogotá, Colombia • **Akiko Nakazawa**, Yokohama Gaigo Business College, Japan • **Adrian Nunn,** EF International School of English, Los Angeles, California, USA • **Margarita Ordaz Mejía**, Universidad Americana de Acapulco, Mexico • **Sherry Ou**, Fu-Jen Catholic University, Taipei, Taiwan • **Thelma Jonas Péres**, Casa Thomas Jefferson, Brasília, Brazil • **Renata Philippov**, Associação Alumni, São Paulo, Brazil • **Ciarán Quinn**, Otemae College, Osaka, Japan • **Ron Ragsdale**, Bilgi University, Istanbul, Turkey • **Luis Ramírez F.,** Instituted Norteamericano de Cultura, Concepción, Chile • **Martha Restrepo Rodríguez**, Politécnico Grancolombiano, Santafé de Bogotá, Colombia • **Irene Reyes Giordanelli**, Centro Cultural Colombo Americano, Santiago de Cali, Colombia • **Dolores Rodríguez**, CELE (Centro de Lenguas), Universidad Autónoma de Puebla, Mexico • **Idia Rodríguez**, University of Puerto Rico-Arecibo, Puerto Rico • **Eddy Rojas & teachers**, Centro de Idiomas de la P. Universidad Católica, Peru • **Ricardo Romero**, Centro Cultural Colombo Americano, Santafé de Bogotá, Colombia • **Blanca Lilia Rosales Bremont**, Universidad Americana de Acapulco, Mexico • **Marie Adele Ryan**, Associação Alumni, São Paulo, Brazil • **Nadia Sarkis**, União Cultural, São Paulo, Brazil • **Andrea Seidel**, Universidad Americana de Acapulco, Mexico • **Hada Shammar**, American Language Center, Amman, Jordan • **Lai Yin Shem**, Centro Colombo Americano, Medellín, Colombia • **Maria Cristina Siqueira**, CEL-LEP, São Paulo, Brazil • **María Inés Sandoval Astudillo**, Instituto Chileno Norteamericano, Chillán, Chile • **Lilian Munhoz Soares**, Centro Cultural Brasil Estados Unidos, Santos, Brazil • **Mário César de Sousa**, Instituto Brazil-Estados Unidos, Fortaleza, Brazil • **Tatiana Suárez,** Politécnico Grancolombiano, Santafé de Bogota, Colombia • **Richard Paul Taylor**, Nagoya University of Commerce and Business Administration, Japan • **David Thompson**, Instituto Mexicano Norteamericano de Relaciones Culturales, Guadalajara, Mexico • **Mr. Uzawa**, Sankei International College, Tokyo, Japan • **Nilda Valdez**, Centro Cultural Salvadoreño, El Salvador • **Euclides Valencia Cepeda**, Universidad Distrital, Santafé de Bogotá, Colombia • **Ana Verde**, American Language Institute, Montevideo, Uruguay • **Andrea Zaidenberg**, Step English Language Center, Argentina.

Preface

True Colors is a complete and articulated five-level adult or young adult course in English as a foreign language. Each book is intended to be completed in a period of 60 to 90 class hours. There are two possible beginning-level entry points: Basic level or Book 1. This Book 2 text follows Book 1.

There are two reasons why this course is entitled *True Colors*. It presents the true voice of the native speaker of American English, and it systematically teaches students to communicate *in their own words*—to **let their true colors shine through.**

Focus and Approach

True Colors is a highly communicative international course enhanced by strong four-skills support, including a two-step listening strand and an abundance of games, info-gaps, and other interactive activities. Within each unit short, integrated social language and grammar lessons ensure concentrated oral practice and production. *True Colors* takes into account different learning and teaching styles. It is centered on task-based strategies and the well-known fact that practice in each skill area enhances mastery of the others.

A major innovation of the *True Colors* series is to systematically build students' ability to present their own ideas, opinions, and feelings—both accurately and confidently. For this reason, every activity leads students to gain ownership of the language, progressively moving them *away* from models

to express thoughts in their own words and to improvise based on what they know.

True Colors carefully distinguishes between receptive and productive language. It consistently presents language in the receptive mode before—and at a slightly higher difficulty level than—the productive mode. Research has shown that students are more successful when they become familiar with new language before having to produce it. For this reason, *True Colors* presents EFL students with a wealth of both receptive and productive models, combining exposure and practice for increased understanding and attainable mastery.

True Colors is specifically designed for use by students who rarely encounter English outside of class. The course is built around a wealth of speaking and reading models of the true voice of the American speaker. This refreshing change from "textbook English" is essential for students who have limited access to real native speech and writing.

Because international students do not have the opportunity to speak to native speakers on a regular basis, *True Colors* does not present activities such as interviewing native speakers or watching TV in English. Instead, the course serves as a replacement for immersion in an English-speaking environment, making the classroom itself a microcosm of the English-speaking world. The goal and promise of *True Colors* is to prepare students to move out of this textbook and to understand, speak, read, and write in the real world.

Student Population

Book 2 of *True Colors* is written for adult and young adult high beginners. It follows *True Colors* Book 1. It has been pilot-tested in classrooms throughout the world and with students of numerous language groups.

Book 4 concludes at a high-intermediate level. The Basic level text is an alternative entry point for very weak false beginners or true beginners.

Course Length

True Colors student's books are designed to cover from 60 to 90 class hours of instruction. Although each student's book is a complete course in itself, giving presentation, practice, and production of all four skills, a full complement of supplementary materials is available to further expand the material.

Components of the Course

Student's Book   The student's book is made up of ten units and two review units, one coming after Unit 5 and another coming after Unit 10.

Teacher's Edition   The teacher's edition is interleaved with full-color student's book pages and contains an introduction to the format and approach of *True Colors*; page-by-page teaching suggestions especially written for the teacher who teaches outside an English-speaking country; tapescripts for the audiocassettes; a complete answer key to the exercises in the student's book, workbook, and achievement tests.

Teacher's Bonus Pack   The Teacher's Bonus Pack is a unique set of reproducible hands-on learning-support activities which include flash cards for large- or small-group vocabulary presentations, pronunciation game cards, duplicating masters that contain photo stories with empty speech balloons for student oral and written improvisation, learner-created grammar notes, and interactive conversation cards for social language reinforcement. The Teacher's Bonus Pack provides suggestions for tailoring *True Colors* to the needs of a variety of settings.

Workbook   The workbook contains numerous additional opportunities for written reinforcement of the language taught in the student's book. The exercises in the workbook are suitable for homework or for classwork.

Audiocassettes   The audiocassettes contain all the receptive models for listening and reading, the conversations, the vocabulary presentations, the Listening with a Purpose texts, the reading texts, and the pronunciation presentations and practices from the student's book. The audiocassettes provide space for student practice and self-correction.

Videocassette   The videocassette, *True Voices,* contains a unique combination of controlled and improvised dramatic episodes that support the social language and grammar in the *True Colors* student's book. In addition, students see a video magazine of scenes depicting the themes touched on throughout the student's book (shopping, working, etc.) and on-the-street interviews about the same topics and themes.

Video Workbook   A video workbook provides active language practice and reinforcement of all social language and grammar from the video.

Achievement Tests   Achievement tests offer opportunities for evaluation of student progress on a unit-by-unit basis. In addition, a placement test is available to aid in placing groups in one of the five levels of *True Colors*: Basic, Book 1, Book 2, Book 3, or Book 4.

Student's Book Unit Contents

Photo Story   An illustrated conversation or story provokes interest, provides enjoyment, and demonstrates the use of target language in authentic, natural speech. This rich model of real speech can be presented as a reading or a listening. It is purposely designed to be a slight step ahead of students' productive ability because students can understand more than they can produce, and the EFL student needs abundant authentic models of native speech.

Comprehension   Questions about the conversation focus on the key comprehension skills of factual recall, confirmation of content, identifying main ideas, drawing conclusions, and understanding meaning from context. These can serve as listening comprehension or reading comprehension exercises.

Social Language and Grammar Lessons
Short, numbered lessons form the instructional core of each unit of *True Colors*. Social language and grammar are tightly linked in each of these mini-lessons, through the following combination of presentations and opportunities for practice:

Conversation   A short dialogue at the students' productive level presents and models important social language.

Pair Practice   The same dialogue is presented for student practice with opportunities for personalization of the social language. This limited opportunity for manipulation is the first step toward ownership of the language that is the goal and promise of *True Colors*.

Vocabulary   Illustrated and captioned vocabulary presentations within each unit provide students with important words to make their own. Students are not asked to guess the meaning of the unit's active vocabulary; instead, *True Colors* presents a clear illustration to convey meaning and follows it with opportunities for practice and free production.

Grammar   Clear, well-explained grammar presentations are integrated with the social language and support comprehension and production of it. These grammar presentations never occur in isolation but rather form a support for the social language of the lesson, giving the grammar both meaning and purpose. To this end, grammar exercises are set in a context that supports the communicative focus of the lesson.

 A major goal of *True Colors* is to teach students to improvise based on the language they already know. Improvisation is the "fifth skill"—the one students need to master in order to move out of the pages of a textbook and into the real world. Through a continuum of freer and freer opportunities for language ownership, *True Colors* students put the course into their own words, **letting their own true colors shine through.**

Pronunciation Each unit isolates a basic and important feature of the pronunciation or intonation of spoken American English. Practice is structured into games and into listening, speaking, and dictation activities.

Game or Info-Gap Each unit contains at least one interactive language activity that activates grammar, social language, vocabulary, or pronunciation.

Listening with a Purpose In addition to the recorded texts in the unit, one or two additional listening texts provide another receptive model a step above students' productive ability. A two-step comprehension syllabus centers on two essential listening skills—determining context and focusing attention. Through a unique and rigorous approach to listening comprehension similar to the reading comprehension skills of skimming and scanning, students build their ability to understand at a level above what is normally expected of high beginners.

Reading Each unit provides practice in the reading skill with texts slightly above students' productive ability. Topics are especially devised to create motivated readers, and each reading is followed by further comprehension practice in all the comprehension subskills.

 This unique and exciting culminating activity systematically builds students' ability to express their own opinions, ideas, and feelings on a variety of topics. Carefully designed questions provoke interest without soliciting production above students' level. Each Heart to Heart activity comes near the end of the unit, ensuring adequate preparation for success.

Writing Writing activities in each unit provide real and realistic writing tasks that reinforce the target language in the writing skill while providing additional opportunities for personal expression.

 This full-page illustration ends each unit and has been especially drawn to elicit from students all the language they have learned with the unit—the vocabulary, the social language, the grammar, and the thematic contexts. Students begin talking about the contents of this picture early in the unit and continue throughout the unit. At the end of the unit, they ask each other questions about the actions depicted, they make true and false statements about what they see, they create conversations for the characters, they tell stories about what is happening—all IN THEIR OWN WORDS. All students, regardless of ability, will succeed at their own levels because what the students know how to say has been drawn into the illustration and what they don't know how to say has been purposely left out.

Review Units These units are provided after Unit 5 (mid-book) and at the end. They provide review, self-tests, extra classroom practice, and a social language self-test.

Appendices The key vocabulary, verb charts, and spelling rules for gerunds and participles are organized and presented at the end of the book for easy reference and test preparation.

About the Authors and Series Director

Authors

Jay Maurer

Jay Maurer has taught English in Binational Centers, colleges, and universities in Portugal, Spain, Mexico, the Somali Republic, and the United States. In addition, he taught intensive English at Columbia University's American Language Program.

Dr. Maurer has an M.A. and an M. Ed. in Applied Linguistics as well as a Ph.D. in The Teaching of English, all from Columbia University. In addition to this new adult and young adult English course, he is the author of the Advanced Level of Longman's widely acclaimed *Focus on Grammar* series and co-author of the three-level *Structure Practice in Context* series. Dr. Maurer teaches and writes in the Seattle, Washington, area and recently conducted a series of teaching workshops in Brazil and Japan.

Irene E. Schoenberg

Irene E. Schoenberg has taught English to international students for over twenty years at Hunter College's International Language Institute and at Columbia University's American Language Program. Additionally, she trains English instructors in EFL/ESL teaching methods at The New School for Social Research. Her M.A. is in TESOL from Columbia University. She is a popular speaker to national and international TESOL groups.

Professor Schoenberg is the author of the Basic Level of the *Focus on Grammar* series as well as the author of the two engaging, unique, and widely used conversation texts, *Talk About Trivia* and *Talk About Values*. In addition to *True Colors*, Professor Schoenberg is developing a new visual dictionary for learners of English.

Series Director

Joan Saslow

Joan Saslow has taught English and foreign languages to adults and young adults in both South America and the United States. She taught English at the Binational Centers of Valparaíso and Viña del Mar, Chile, and English and French at the Catholic University of Valparaíso. She taught English as a Foreign Language to Japanese university students at Marymount College and to international students in Westchester Community College's intensive program.

Ms. Saslow is the author of *English in Context: Reading Comprehension for Science and Technology,* a three-level text series. In addition, Ms. Saslow has been an editor of language teaching materials, a teacher trainer, and a frequent speaker at gatherings of English teachers outside the United States for twenty-five years.

I was thinking of asking Kate out.

Warm up: *Read the speech in the first and last pictures. What do you think happened? Read or listen.* 🎧

* *This word is very informal and rude. Americans don't use it in polite conversation.*

Comprehension: Confirming Content

*Mark the following statements **true, false,** or **I don't know.***

		True	False	I don't know.
Example:	Tim wants to ask Kate out.	☑	☐	☐
1.	At first, Kate doesn't remember Tim.	☐	☐	☐
2.	Kate likes to dissect frogs.	☐	☐	☐
3.	Kate was a good biology student.	☐	☐	☐
4.	Tim is happy he called Kate.	☐	☐	☐

HOW TO **express location/get reacquainted/express greetings**

Vocabulary • Expressions of Location

🎧 *Look at the pictures. Say each phrase.*

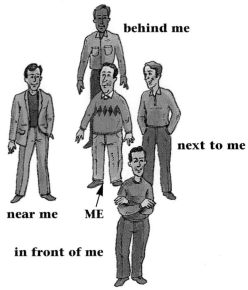

behind me

next to me

near me   **ME**

in front of me

Conversation

🎧 *Read and listen to the conversation.*

A: I don't know if you remember me. My name is Charlie Mann.
B: Sure I remember you. You sat next to me.
A: Yeah, that's right. How are you doing?
B: Fine. Nice to see you again.

🎧 *Listen again and practice.*

Vocabulary • Greetings and Responses

🎧 *Say each greeting and response.*

How are you doing?
How's it going?
How are you?

Nice to see you again.
Glad to see you.
Great to see you.

Fine.
OK.
Great.

Nice to see you, too.

Pair Practice

Practice the conversation and vocabulary with a partner. Use your own words.

A: I don't know if you remember me. My

name is _____.

B: Sure I remember you. You _____.

A: Yeah, that's right. _____?

B: _____.

✓ **Now you know how to get reacquainted with someone.**

 **Look at the first picture on page 13. With a partner, create a conversation for one of the pairs of people. Use your own words.**

SOCIAL LANGUAGE AND GRAMMAR 2

How to **tell a story about the past**

The Past Continuous and the Simple Past Tense

The past continuous shows an action that was in progress in the past. Form the past continuous with **was** or **were** and the present participle.

> present participle
> I **was sleeping** at ten o'clock last night.

Use the simple past tense to show an action that occurred one time and then stopped.

> The telephone **rang** at ten o'clock.

Use the past continuous and the simple past tense to show one event interrupting an action in progress.

action in progress (past continuous)	one event (simple past tense)
I **was sleeping**	when the telephone **rang**.

GRAMMAR TASK: Find three sentences with the past continuous in the photo story on pages 2–3.

Grammar in a Context

Complete the sentences. Use the simple past tense or the past continuous.

Grandson: Grandpa, how _____

you and Grandma first _____?
         1. meet

Grandfather: Well, let's see.... We _____
         2. meet

fifty years ago at an ice-cream parlor.

I _____ a waiter there. When
   3. be

your Grandma _____ in, I _____
       4. walk   **5.** wash

the counter. She _____
       6. babysit

her younger sisters. She _____ an ice-cream sundae for them to share.
         7. order

Pretty soon they _____ to argue about the sundae.
       8. start

Grandson: And then what _____?
       9. happen

Grandfather: Well, her sisters _____ about sharing the ice-cream sundae when it
      10. argue

_____ on the floor. I _____ them another sundae and
 11. fall   **12.** bring

_____ Grandma out to the movies.
  13. invite

Grandson: _____ you _____ her to marry you when you were at the movies?
         14. ask

Grandfather: No, not that day. But about six months later I did.

Improvise

Many Americans who were alive in 1969 like to remember and talk about the first astronaut landing on the moon.

With your class, think of an important news story you remember. Talk about what you were doing when you heard the news.

☑ **Now you know how to tell a story about the past.**

Pronunciation

/ʃ/ and /tʃ/

🎧 *Look at the pictures. Say these words.*

wash   **watch**

wish   **witch**

share   **chair**

🎧 *Now listen to the sentences. Circle the correct picture in each pair.*

Pair Practice

Now work with a partner. Describe one of the pictures above. Your partner points to the picture you describe.

Reading

An Article from a Business Magazine

*Before You Read: Think about this question: Is the office a good place to fall in love?
Read the article.*

Business Digest

Love at the Office

by Kathleen Young

Alyssa first met Josh at work. He was giving a talk at a meeting when Alyssa walked in, twenty minutes late. He was a little annoyed at her lateness. However, after that first meeting, they started to work on projects together.

Alyssa says, "We were a wonderful team. We respected and learned from each other. When we had to stay late, we began having dinners together. We became good friends. Soon we hated being apart." After a year, Josh proposed. Alyssa and Josh are celebrating their second anniversary next Monday.

Today, 46 percent of the workforce in the United States is female. More and more women are becoming top executives, both in the United States and around the world. In many offices, men and women work side by side as equals. In many ways, the workplace is becoming a community whose members share work projects and interests. And love grows naturally in places where people share interests and work.

Alyssa and Josh are an example of why an office romance can be a very good thing. Their love and their interest in each other increased their interest in their work. Their romance ended up being good for their company and for them as well.

Comprehension: Understanding Meaning from Context

Circle the choice closer in meaning to each underlined word or phrase.

1. He was a little <u>annoyed</u> at her lateness.

   a. angry   **b.** interested

2. We <u>became good friends</u>.

   a. were always good friends   **b.** were good friends after some time passed

3. After a year, Josh <u>proposed</u>.

   a. asked Alyssa to marry him   **b.** asked Alyssa to work for him

4. Alyssa and Josh are an example of why an office <u>romance</u> can be a very good thing.

   a. business relationship   **b.** love relationship

5. Their love and their interest in each other <u>increased their interest in their work</u>.

   a. made their interest in their work grow   **b.** hurt their interest in their work

Grammar in a Context • Verb Tense Review

*Read this second case study of love at work from **Business Digest**.*
Complete the sentences with the correct form of the verb.

Sue and Ed are lawyers at the same firm. They _____ on Ed's first day at
                                                    1. meet

the company five months ago. Ed _____ for a book when several books
                                     2. reach

_____ on the floor. Everyone _____ up, and Ed _____ embarrassed.
3. fall   **4. look**   **5. feel**

Sue _____ him replace the books. After that they _____ friends.
      6. help   **7. become**

Now Sue and Ed _____ lunch together on workdays. They _____ out
                   8. have   **9. go**

almost every Saturday night. Next month they are going to Boston on a business

trip. Sue's family _____ in Boston, and Sue _____ Boston well. Ed
                      10. be   **11. know**

_____ Boston at all, so Sue _____ him all her favorite places and
12. know / not   **13. show**

introduce him to her family.

For Sue and Ed, "romance and work" are a great mix. Sue says, "Right now

Ed and I _____ very hard, but we _____ every minute."
            14. work   **15. love**

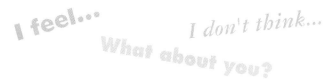

Talk to a partner about love relationships. Compare your opinions.

Why do you think one person begins to love another person?

Do men and women look for different things in a relationship?

How are office romances good? Can they cause problems?

Listening with a Purpose

Focus Attention

Mitch and Sheila are guests at an engagement party for Andrea and Bill, who are going to get married in two months.

🎧 *Listen to their conversation. Make notes about facts.*
🎧 *Now listen again and write three facts about Mitch.*

SOCIAL LANGUAGE AND GRAMMAR 3

How to make an invitation/accept or decline an invitation

Vocabulary • Social Activities

🎧 *Look at the pictures. Say each phrase.*

have coffee   **have dinner**   **see a movie**   **go to the beach**   **study together**

Conversation 1

🎧 *Read and listen to the conversation.*

A: How'd you like to have dinner tonight?
B: I'd love to. What time?
A: Seven o'clock?
B: Great. Where shall we meet?
A: At Spiro's Restaurant?
B: That's fine. See you later.

🎧 *Listen again and practice.*

Vocabulary • Ways to Accept an Invitation

🎧 *Read each word or phrase.*

Pair Practice

Practice the conversation and vocabulary with a partner. Use your own words.

A: How'd you like to _____?

B: _____. What time?

A: _____?

B: _____. Where shall we meet?

A: At _____?

B: _____. See you later.

☑ **Now you know how to invite someone to do something.
You also know how to accept an invitation.**

The Present Continuous and Have To for Future Actions

I'm *working* this weekend.	I *have to* study on Sunday.

Conversation 2

🎧 *Read and listen to the conversation.*

A: I was wondering.... Would you like to have coffee sometime this weekend?
B: Well, actually, I'm working this weekend.
A: That's too bad.
B: Maybe some other time?
A: OK.

🎧 *Listen again and practice.*

Vocabulary • Present and Future Time Expressions

🎧 *Look at the calendars and planners. Say each word or phrase.*

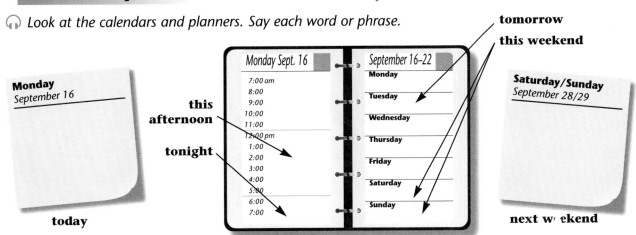

tomorrow

this weekend

Monday
September 16

**this
afternoon**

tonight

Monday Sept. 16	September 16–22
7:00 am	**Monday**
8:00	
9:00	**Tuesday**
10:00	
11:00	**Wednesday**
12:00 pm	
1:00	**Thursday**
2:00	
3:00	**Friday**
4:00	
5:00	**Saturday**
6:00	
7:00	**Sunday**

Saturday/Sunday
September 28/29

today

next weekend

Pair Practice

Practice the conversation and vocabulary with a partner. Use your own words.

A: I was wondering.... Would you like to _____?

B: Well, actually, I _____.

A: That's too bad.

B: Maybe some other time?

A: _____.

☑ **Now you know another way to invite someone to do something. You also know how to decline an invitation.**

Writing
Short Notes in Response to Ads

Here are some ads from the local newspaper. Some are for part-time work. Some are for friendship or romance.

Choose one of these people and write a short note of response. It can be funny or serious.

English professor. Looking for part-time graduate assistant to grade tests during exam week. Box 276.

Young couple needs part-time babysitter at beach house. Four energetic children, 2, 4, 7, and 13. All meals included. Lots of time off. Box 547.

Handsome banker. Interests include skiing, music, family, and food. I'm looking for a happy woman with a great sense of humor and a big appetite. Box 244.

Romantic 60-year-old female dog trainer. Loves the theater, movies, music, and walks on the beach. Looking for a lively, intelligent, and athletic gentleman. If you have the same interests, please write me at box 331.

Friendly, fun-loving, middle-aged English-speaking couple traveling in Thailand. Need interpreter with a current driver's license, available July and August. Box 222.

Elderly retired army officer. Seeking companion and chess partner. Box 722.

Example:

Box 244
To the "handsome banker":
I read your ad in the newspaper. I am a happy woman. I love to eat and to cook. I am friendly, and I have a big, friendly family. Would you like to meet to have coffee sometime soon? I'm enclosing a photo of myself and my family.
You can call me at 534-2231.
Talk to you soon!

Warm up: Talk about this picture with a partner.
• What is the date and time? • Where are these people?
• Who are they? • What are they doing? • What are they saying?

Then: Create a conversation for the couple in the second picture.
OR Invent a story about these people. What does he want to do?
What is she thinking? Say as much as you can.

How many will, and how many won't?

Warm up: Look at the pictures. Where are these people?
Read or listen. 🎧

Walk on black squares only.
Do not walk on white squares.

OK. Now imagine this experiment.
You're in a supermarket, and the
floor is black and white squares.

There's a sign that says
WALK ON BLACK SQUARES ONLY.
DO NOT WALK ON WHITE SQUARES.

Out of a hundred people, how many will obey, and
how many won't? What's your prediction? . . .
Vicky, what do you think? Will they stay on the
black squares?

Well . . . I don't think very
many will obey the sign. Maybe
about twenty or thirty.

No, I think a lot more will.
Maybe about seventy.
People are like sheep.

DO NOT
TOUCH
THIS BOX

OK. Now, imagine another
experiment. There's a sign
on a box that says
DO NOT TOUCH THIS BOX.

How many people will touch it,
and how many won't?

Comprehension: Understanding Meaning from Context

Circle the choice closest in meaning to each underlined word or phrase.

1. How many will <u>obey</u>, and how many won't?

    a. do what someone tells them to do   **b.** do something good   **c.** do something bad

2. People <u>are like sheep</u>.

    a. do what others do   **b.** don't do what others do   **c.** are crazy

3. They won't touch it if someone's watching, but most people will if <u>no one's around</u>.

    a. no one touches it   **b.** no one's a police officer   **c.** no one's there

4. Will we ever <u>get to</u> do an experiment like that in this class?

    a. want to   **b.** like to   **c.** have the opportunity to

HOW TO **talk about the future/ask for a favor/offer help**

Will as Future

Use *will* or *will not* plus the base form to talk about the future.

> I don't think it *will rain* today. It *will not rain* tomorrow either.

Contract *will* to *'ll*. Contract *will not* to *won't*.

> I*'ll* be at the party, but Dorothy *won't*.

Look at these short answers with *will*.

> Yes, *she will*.   No, *she won't*.

TIPS: Do not contract *will* in the affirmative short answer.

> *Will* never has *-s* in the third-person singular.

To make questions with *will*, invert *will* and the subject.

> *Will it* rain today?
>
> When *will you* be there?

Remember these other ways to talk about the future.

> with *be going to*: I*'m going to visit* my aunt and uncle this summer.
>
> with the present continuous: We*'re having* dinner at Sam and Jane's house tonight.

GRAMMAR TASK: Find three examples with *will* or *won't* in the photo story on pages 14–15.

Grammar in a **C**ontext

William and Sandra are at the supermarket. They are doing the experiment.

Complete the conversation with **will**, **won't**, *or* **'ll**. *Use the contraction with a pronoun whenever possible.*

> OK, here's our first subject. _____ he touch the box?
> **1.**

> Yes, he _____. He's a tough guy.
> **2.**
> He doesn't look obedient.

> You're right.

In Your Own Words Look at the picture on page 25. Create a conversation for the two students. Use your own words.

Conversation

🎧 *Read and listen to the conversation.*

A: Hello?

B: Hi, Joan. This is Irene. Can you do me a favor?

A: Sure. What's up?

B: Can you drive me to the dentist's office this afternoon?

A: Sure, be glad to.

B: Thanks a lot. I'll return the favor sometime.

🎧 *Listen again and practice.*

Vocabulary • Everyday Favors We Do for Others

Look at the pictures. Say each phrase.

buy some groceries

mail some letters

drive (a person) to (a place)

take some clothes to the cleaner

wait for a delivery

Pair Practice

Practice the conversation and vocabulary with a partner. Use your own words.

A: Hello?

B: Hi, _____. This is _____. Can you do me a favor?

A: Sure. What's up?

B: _____?

A: Sure, be glad to.

B: Thanks a lot. I'll return the favor sometime.

☑ **Now you know how to ask someone for a favor. You also know how to offer help.**

A Visitor from the Year 3001

*(future with **will**—more practice)*

Partner B is a time traveler from 3001.

Partner A, use the cues on this chart to ask Partner B questions about the year 3001.

Partner B, turn to page 144 for the answers.

Then, for questions 6–10, Partner A is the time traveler.

TIP: In the future, ***there is*** and ***there are*** become ***there will be***.

Partner A's Cues

1. there / be / a cure for AIDS?

2. computers / control everything?

3. people / live / on other planets?

4. there / be / enough food and water?

5. there / be / electric cars?

6. No / won't.

a panda

7. Yes / will.

a robot

8. Yes / will.

a solar-
powered house

9. No / won't.

10. No / won't.

Bonus Question: Do you agree with the answers?

Receptive Model

Listening with a Purpose

Focus Attention

Read the assignment for Dr. Vance's class.

🎧 *Listen to the conversation between two students. Listen for the predictions the male student makes. As you listen, circle his predictions on the chart below.*

Dr. Vance   Social Psychology 101
Extra Credit Assignment

Assignment: Go to the intersection of Highway 78 and Cook Road in the evening when there is very little traffic. There is a traffic light at this intersection. Count the number of cars that stop for the red light and the number that ___'t stop. Don't let the drivers see you, and choose cars only when there are no other cars nearby.

Cars	Predictions	Results
Car 1: red Honda	will / won't stop	stops / doesn't stop
Car 2: white Volvo	will / won't stop	stops / doesn't stop
Car 3: red Ford	will / won't stop	stops / doesn't stop
Car 4: green Jeep	will / won't stop	stops / doesn't stop

🎧 *Now listen again for the results. Circle the results on the chart.*

Heart to Heart

I think...
In my opinion...
because...

With a partner, make a list of laws and rules. Here are some examples:

laws	rules
You have to have a driver's license to drive a car.	*You have to wear a uniform to some schools.*

Now compare your opinions.

Is it always necessary to obey rules? Laws?
Do you obey all the laws and rules on your list?

I feel...
I don't think...
What about you?

SOCIAL LANGUAGE AND GRAMMAR 2

How to express willingness and refusal

Will and Won't for Willingness and Refusal

Dad, I can't fix my car. **Will** you help me with it? (willingness)

I've really got a problem. My kids **won't** eat vegetables. (refusal)

Grammar in a Context

*Complete the conversations with **will** or **won't**. Contract **will** to '**ll** if it occurs with a pronoun.*

I don't know what to do. Jennifer _____ eat
                                          1.
meat, and Bobby _____ eat vegetables.
                        2.
They're both going to die of malnutrition!

You think you've got it bad! Teddy _____ only
                                            3.
eat cereal, ice cream, and bananas. Nothing else.

I can see it all now. I'll say, "Laura, _____ you
                                                4.
marry me and move to Kansas?" She'll say, "Of
course, darling. What took you so long to ask?"

Hmm. You need a reality check.
She _____ marry you, all right. But I'm
          5.
betting she _____ move to Kansas.
                    6.

Vocabulary • Fruits and Vegetables

🎧 *Look at the pictures. Say each word.*

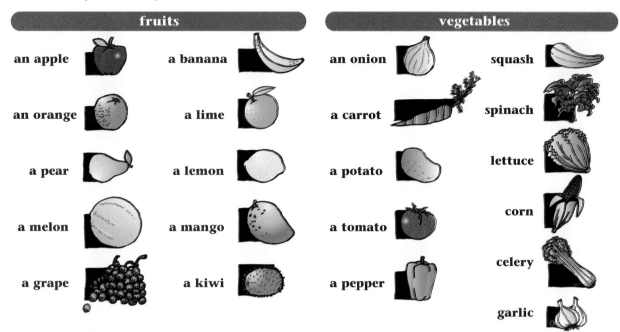

fruits			vegetables	
an apple	a banana	an onion	squash	
an orange	a lime	a carrot	spinach	
a pear	a lemon	a potato	lettuce	
a melon	a mango	a tomato	corn	
a grape	a kiwi	a pepper	celery	
			garlic	

In Your Own Words — **Look at the picture on page 25. How many fruits and vegetables can you name? Tell your partner which foods you will or won't eat.**

☑ **Now you know how to talk about willingness.**

Receptive Model

Listening with a Purpose

Focus Attention

🎧 *Listen to the conversation about willingness. Then mark the following statements **true** or **false**.*

	True	False
1. Mary will take Andy downtown.	☐	☐
2. Andy will take Mary downtown.	☐	☐
3. Greg will take Andy downtown.	☐	☐

Improvise

🎧 *Listen to the conversation again. Then improvise a similar conversation with a partner. Use your own words.*

In Your Own Words Look at the picture on page 25. With a partner, create a conversation for the mother and the child. Use your own words.

Receptive Model

Reading

A Class Discussion

Before You Read: Think about why people obey orders. Read the discussion.

Obedience

Dr. Vance and his students continue their study of obedience. Dr. Vance wants his students to repeat a famous scientific experiment about obeying orders. The students will pretend to be subjects in the experiment. Here is a transcript of their classroom discussion.

Vance: OK. We want to know if people will do what a leader tells them to do.

Barbara: How will we do that?

Vance: Do you all see this button?

Barbara: Yes. What does it do?

Vance: Well, actually, nothing. But the subjects won't know. I'm going to tell them that if they press the button, you'll get an electric shock. We want to see if the subjects will do what a leader tells them.

Mike: Give us a shock? No way! That'll hurt!

Vance: No. You weren't paying attention. Remember: The button doesn't do anything. I'll just tell the subjects it'll give you a shock. It won't be the truth.

Mike: So what's the point?

Vance: We want to know two things. First, will the subjects actually obey and give you a shock? Second, will they continue to give you a shock if they think the shock causes a lot of pain?

Mike: But it won't hurt because there won't be a shock, right?

Vance: Right. You'll have to pretend.

Barbara: What actually happened in the original experiment?

Vance: Most subjects obeyed and gave the shocks. What do you think this tells us about people?

Barbara: It sounds like people are too willing to obey leaders.

Mike: I think this experiment is terrible.

Vance: Hmm. A lot of people thought the original experiment was wrong, too.

Comprehension: Factual Recall

*Mark the following statements **true** or **false**.*

	True	False
1. Dr. Vance's class is studying obedience.	☐	☐
2. Mike wants to get a shock.	☐	☐
3. The button will give the students a shock.	☐	☐
4. The students will have to pretend.	☐	☐
5. Mike doesn't like the experiment.	☐	☐

Comprehension: Interpretation and Analysis

You are a subject in Dr. Vance's experiment. Will you press the button?

Pronunciation
/v/ and /w/

Look at the pictures. Say these words.

/v/		/w/	
vest	Stan is wearing a **vest**.	**west**	The arrow is pointing **west**.
vent	Open the heating **vent**.	**went**	She **went** into the house.
verse	A **verse** is a part of a poem.	**worse**	The first score is bad, but the second score is **worse**.
vet	Vicky took her cat to the **vet**.	**wet**	Everything is **wet**.

Listen again and repeat.

Dictation

🎧 *You will hear the words from the list on page 23. Write each word you hear.*

1. _____

2. _____

3. _____

4. _____

5. _____

6. _____

7. _____

8. _____

9. _____

10. _____

Bonus Sentence:

11. _____

Writing
A Paragraph

The Year 3001

Look back at the Info-Gap on pages 18–19. Imagine that you are a visitor from the year 3001. Write a paragraph about what life is like.

Use the Info-Gap questions and answers as a guide. Indent the first sentence.

indent ➤

> I am a visitor from the year 3001. Let me tell you what life is like. First, most people have robots in their homes. And

Warm up: Talk about this scene with a partner. • Where are the students? • What are they studying? • Where are they standing? • Who are they watching? • What will happen?

Then: Create conversations for all the people. OR Tell a story. Say as much as you can.

25

It's the softest leather in the world.

Warm up: Look at the pictures. What do you think the people are talking about? Read or listen.

Hey, John, look at that jacket. Nice, huh?

Come on. Let's go in and ask.

Yeah. It must cost a fortune. Forget it, Bill.

Oh. The black leather one. Here. Let me show it to you.

May I help you?

You mean the brown jacket?

No, the other one.

Yes. I was wondering. . . . How much is that jacket in the window?

How much is it?

Only $495.

Comprehension: Confirming Content

*Mark the following statements **true**, **false**, or **I don't know**.*

	True	False	I don't know.
1. Bill thinks the black leather jacket is expensive.	☐	☐	☐
2. The black leather jacket is the most expensive jacket in the store.	☐	☐	☐
3. Bill's friend John wants Bill to buy the jacket.	☐	☐	☐
4. The salesperson thinks that Bill wants the girls to like him.	☐	☐	☐

HOW TO compare people, places, and things/ask for and give clarification

The Comparative Form of Adjectives

Compare two people, places, or things with the comparative form of adjectives. Follow these rules.

Add *-er* to one-syllable and some two-syllable adjectives.

small, quiet	This restaurant is **smaller** and **quieter.**

Put **more** or **less** before most adjectives of two or more syllables.

That ring is **more beautiful.** But it's **less expensive.**

For one-syllable or two-syllable adjectives that end in **y**, change the **y** to **i** and add *-er*.

easy	That's an **easier** book.

Look at these irregular comparatives.

good → better	bad → worse	far → farther

T I P : Use **than** to give more information.

The sofas are **cheaper than the chairs.**

GRAMMAR TASK: Find an adjective in the comparative form in the photo story on pages 26-27.

In Your Own Words Look at the picture on page 37. With a partner, compare the two sweaters. Use your own words.

Grammar in a Context

Complete the conversation with the comparative form of the adjectives.

So what are you going to have?

I can't decide between the salad and the pasta.

You mean the pasta Alfredo? Have the salad. They put tons of cream in the pasta Alfredo. The salad is _____.
1. healthy

I know, but the pasta is a lot _____.
2. good

Grammar with a Partner

Look at these two ads for Quality Airlines.

*With a partner, compare the ads. Which one is better? Use the following adjectives. You can use **more** or **less**.*

colorful	**pretty**
good	**helpful**
interesting	**long**

Compare your opinions. Explain your reasons.

Look for Quality When You Fly

- Why is Quality Airlines safer than all other airlines?
  All our pilots have more than five years' experience.

- Why is Quality Airlines more comfortable than all other airlines?
  All our seats are designed for comfort.

- Why is the service on Quality Airlines better than on all other airlines?
  All our employees own stock in Quality Airlines.

QUALITY AIRLINES: The Be~~tt~~er *only* Way to Fly

Conversation

🎧 *Read and listen to the conversation.*

A: Excuse me. How much is that jacket in the window?

B: You mean the blue jacket?

A: Yes—the longer one.

B: It's $55.

A: Do you have it in medium?

B: Just a minute. I'll check.

A: Thanks.

🎧 *Listen again and practice.*

Vocabulary • Clothing Sizes

🎧 *Look at the pictures. Say each word or phrase.*

Small   Medium   Large   Extra Large   Petite   Size 8 Regular

Vocabulary • Clothing Materials

🎧 *Look at the pictures. Say each word.*

wool   **cotton**   **nylon**

denim   **fur**   **leather**

Pair Practice

Practice the conversation and vocabulary with a partner. Use your own words.

A: Excuse me. How much is _____ in the window?

B: You mean the _____?

A: Yes—the _____.

B: It's _____.

A: Do you have it in _____?

B: _____.

A: _____.

☑ **Now you know how to ask for and give clarification.**

Pronunciation

Rising Intonation to Clarify

🎧 *Listen and repeat.*

A: She found a desk.
B: A desk?
A: Yes.

A: They went to Bloom's Department Store.
B: Bloom's?
A: Uh-huh.

A: She gave all her money to George.
B: George? You're kidding.
A: No, I'm not.

Now work with a partner. Create conversations for the four items below.
Partner A begins items 1 and 2. Then Partner B begins items 3 and 4. Use your own words.

Example:
      A: I need a jacket.
      B: A jacket?
      A: Uh-huh.

1. A: She bought _____.

    B: _____?

    A: _____.

2. A: They were walking on _____.

    B: _____?

    A: _____.

3. B: He found _____.

    A: _____?

    B: _____.

4. B: He spent _____.

    A: _____?

    B: _____.

In Your Own Words

Look at the picture on page 37. With a partner, create a conversation for the woman and the salesperson about the blouse. Use your own words.

SOCIAL LANGUAGE AND GRAMMAR 2

HOW TO **exchange something in a store/state a problem**

Conversation

🎧 *Read and listen to the conversation.*

A: How can I help you?
B: I need to exchange these boots. They don't fit. They're too tight.
A: Would you like to see them in another size?
B: Yes, please. Do you have them in size eight?
A: Yes, we do. Just a moment. I'll get them for you.
B: Thank you.

🎧 *Listen again and practice.*

Vocabulary • Problems with Fit

Look at the pictures. Say each phrase.

| too tight | too loose | too small | too big | too short |

TIP: Use *too* to give adjectives a negative meaning.

Pair Practice

Practice the conversation and vocabulary with a partner. Use your own words.

A: How can I help you?

B: I need to exchange _____. _____ fit. _____.

A: Would you like to see _____ in another size?

B: Yes, please. Do you _____?

A: _____.

B: _____.

☑ **Now you know how to exchange something in a store and state a problem.**

Improvise

Have a two-part conversation with a partner. First buy something in a store. It could be clothing or something else. Find a problem with the item.

Now bring the item back to the store and exchange it for something else. Use your own words.

HOW TO **compare things (more practice)**

The Superlative Form of Adjectives

Use the superlative form of adjectives to compare three or more people, places, or things. Follow these rules.

Put **the** before the adjective and add **-est** to one-syllable and some two-syllable adjectives.

cheap | That was **the cheapest** hotel.

Put **the most** or **the least** before most adjectives of two or more syllables.

He bought **the most beautiful** but **the least expensive** tie in the store.

For one-syllable and two-syllable adjectives that end in **y**, put **the** before the adjective, change the **y** to **i**, and add **-est.**

happy | **The happiest** person has the biggest smile of all.

Look at these irregular adjectives.

good → better → the best   bad → worse → the worst   far → farther → the farthest

GRAMMAR TASK: Find an adjective in the superlative form in the photo story on pages 26-27.

Grammar with a Partner

Partner A, complete these questions. Partner B, complete the questions on page 34.
Then exchange papers. Check your partner's work. Answers are on page 144.

Example: (large) ___The Pacific Ocean___ is __the largest__ ocean in the world.
The Pacific Ocean / The Atlantic Ocean / The Indian Ocean

Partner A's questions:

(hot) **1.** _____ is _____ planet in the Solar System.
Venus / Mars / Mercury

(common)* **2.** _____ is _____ word in conversational English.
Me / I / My

(small) **3.** _____ is _____ continent in the world.
Africa / South America / Australia

(heavy) **4.** The _____ is _____ mammal in the world.
whale / elephant / hippopotamus

(busy) **5.** _____ is _____ of these three airports.
Chicago's O'Hare / London's Heathrow / New York's JFK

* Common has two superlative forms: **most common** and **commonest.**

Partner B's questions:

(fast)   **6.** _____ is _____ planet in the Solar System.
          Venus / Mars / Mercury

(common) * **7.** _____ is _____ word in written English.
          The / A / An

(high)   **8.** _____ are _____ mountain range in the world.
          The Alps / The Himalayas / The Rockies

(large)   **9.** _____ is _____ sea in the world.
          The Mediterranean Sea / The South China Sea / The Black Sea

(tall)   **10.** The _____ is _____ animal in the world.
          flamingo / ostrich / giraffe

* **Common** has two superlative forms: **most common** and **commonest.**

Receptive Model

Listening with a Purpose

Focus Attention

🎧 *Listen to this conversation between a customer and a salesperson. Then listen again, focusing on what the salesperson says. He gives several reasons to buy something. Write each reason you hear.*

Receptive Model

Reading
A Business Letter

Before You Read: *Think about what makes a good salesperson.*

Read the story. 🎧

Not long ago, there was a vacancy for a sales position at The Wrap, a clothing store. In response to the ad, a woman wrote the following letter.

Personnel Department
The Wrap
3301 South Elm Street
Mount Kisco, New York 10549

Dear Sir or Madam:

I am writing in response to your advertisement for a sales position at The Wrap. Presently I am working in the luggage department of Bloom's Department Store. It's at 545 Main Street, Flushing, New York. You can judge my sales ability by coming to the store any time you like and pretending to want some luggage.

I am the only one in that department with bright red hair. I will talk to you the same way I talk to all customers. I won't be more helpful or more polite. I won't be friendlier, more patient, or more considerate. Since I won't know you, I won't be able to put on a show for you as my future employer.

I hope to hear from you soon.

Sincerely,

Helen Townsend

Helen Townsend

There were almost a thousand applicants. The red-haired woman got the job.

Three things are helpful in finding a job. First, you need to show your employers that you have initiative, that you are not afraid to try something new. Second, you need to let them know that you have the qualities they are looking for. Finally, you need to show them that you will always try your hardest, even when no one is watching.

The woman with red hair got the job because she did those three important things. First of all, her approach was unique. Her letter was unlike the usual letter to a future employer. Second, she had qualities important in a sales position: helpfulness, friendliness, consideration, and good manners. And finally, when her future employers came to Bloom's Department Store and she didn't know who they were, she treated them very well. She kept her word.

Comprehension: Identifying the Main Idea

Choose another title for this reading.

   a. "Women Make Better Salespeople"   b. "Hair Color"   c. "Success in Today's Job Market"

Comprehension: Understanding Meaning from Context

Circle the choice closer in meaning to each underlined word or phrase.

1. Not long ago, there was a <u>vacancy</u> for a sales position at The Wrap.
   a. job opening   b. vacation

2. I won't be able <u>to put on a show for you</u> as my future employer.
   a. act in a special way for you   b. show you my work

3. Her <u>approach</u> was unique.
   a. technique   b. hair

Heart to Heart

I think...

In my opinion...

because...

Talk to a partner about salespeople. Compare your opinions.

Some salespeople are honest, like the red-haired woman. Some are dishonest, like the sweater salesman in Listening with a Purpose on page 34.

Talk about good and bad salespeople. Give examples from your own experience.

I feel...

I don't think...

What about you?

Writing

A Business Letter

You want your city or your country to be the site of a future Olympics.

In groups of three or four students, write letters to the International Olympic Committee. Try to convince them to choose your city or country to be the site of the Olympics. Give reasons. Use adjectives in comparative and superlative forms. Begin your letter this way:

April 4

International Olympic Committee
Vidy 1
Olympic House
1007 Lausanne, Switzerland

Dear Sir or Madam:

We are writing you from _____. We

would like you to consider _____ for the

Olympics in _____ because it is the most

In Your Own Words

Warm up: *Talk about this scene with a partner.*
- *Where is it?* • *How many items can you name?*
- *Describe them.* • *Compare them.*

Then: *Create conversations for the people. OR Tell a story. Say as much as you can.*

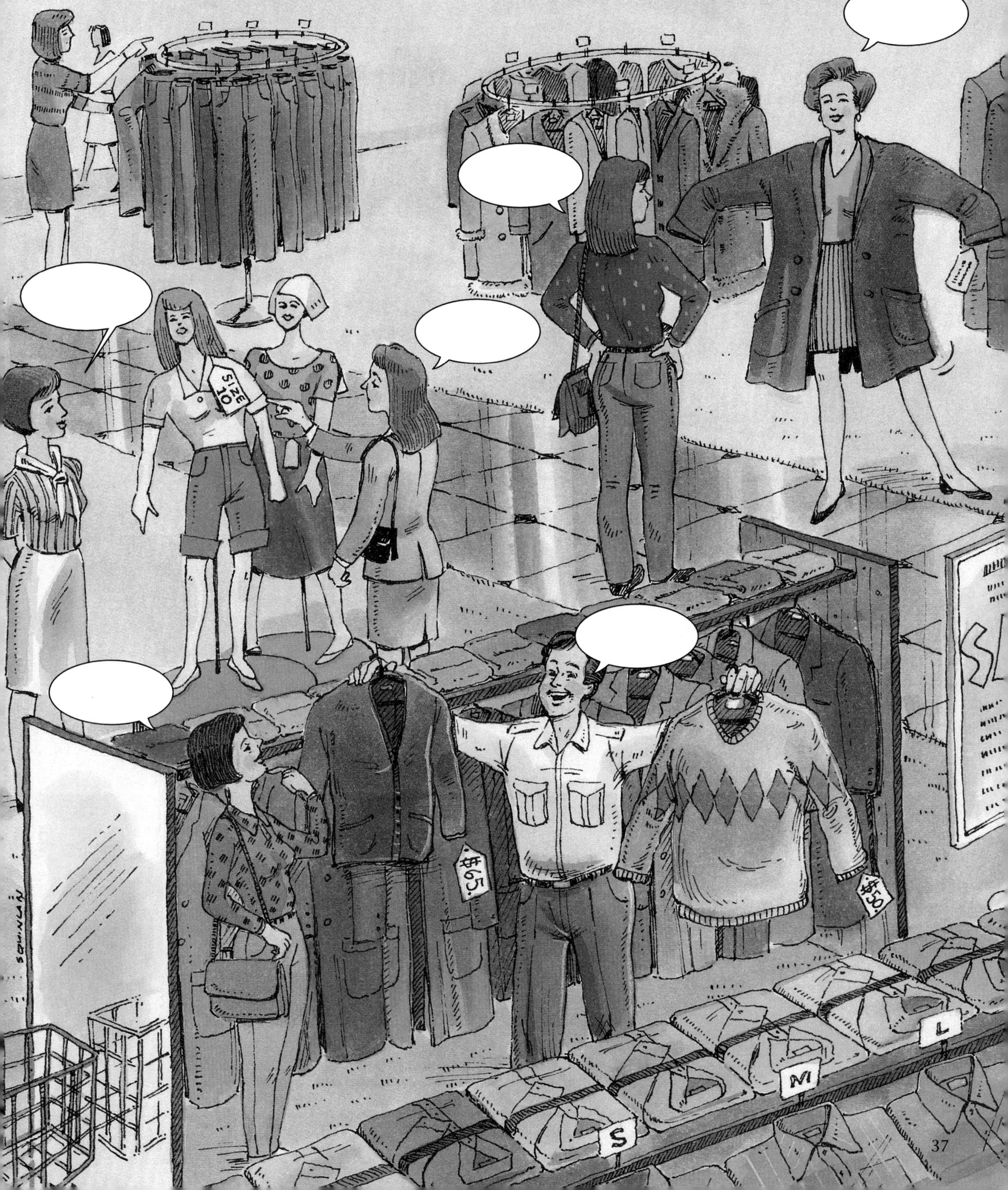

SIZE 10
$65
$50
S
M
L

Receptive Model

Warm up: What do you do when you have a stomachache or a cold?
Read or listen. 🎧

Hello?

Hello, Tom? Lynn. Where have you been? I haven't seen you for days.

I've been sick as a dog since Monday.

Gee, I'm really sorry to hear that. What's wrong?

I've had a terrible stomachache all week.

Have you been to the doctor?

Not yet.

Well, have you tried a ginger ale and rice diet?

What?

Just eat rice and drink ginger ale. It really works.

You're kidding.

Comprehension: Confirming Content

*Mark the following statements **true**, **false**, or **I don't know.***

	True	False	I don't know.
1. Tom has a dog.	☐	☐	☐
2. Tom and Lynn work at the same place.	☐	☐	☐
3. The ginger ale and rice diet doesn't help Tom.	☐	☐	☐

Comprehension: Understanding Meaning from Context

Circle the choice closer in meaning to each sentence.

1. I've been sick as a dog since Monday.

    a. My dog has been sick since Monday.   **b.** I've been very sick since Monday.

2. I think I'm coming down with something.

    a. I think I'm getting sick.   **b.** I think I'm doing too much work.

HOW TO **talk about illness/ask about someone's absence/ offer sympathy**

The Present Perfect—Meaning

Use the present perfect for actions that began in the past and continue into the present.
Compare the present perfect and the simple past tense.

present perfect

I **have had** a backache for two days. (I still have a backache.)

simple past

I **had** a backache for two days. (I don't have a backache anymore.)

Use **for** to show a period of time.

I've had this cold **for six days.**

Use **since** to show a particular time when an action began.

I've had this cold **since Sunday.**

GRAMMAR TASK: Find and circle examples of sentences with **for** and **since** in the photo story on pages 38-39.

Conversation

🎧 *Read and listen to the conversation.*

A: Hello?

B: Hi, Alan? Where have you been? I haven't seen you for days.

A: Well, I've been sick since Monday.

B: Oh, no. What's wrong?

A: I've had a terrible backache all week.

B: I'm sorry to hear that. Hope you feel better soon.

A: Thanks, Pam.

🎧 *Listen again and practice.*

Vocabulary • Ailments

🎧 *Look at the pictures. Say the name of each ailment.*

a sore throat   **a stomachache**   **a rash**

a headache   **a toothache**   **a cough**

a fever   **a cold**   **the flu**

Vocabulary • Questions about Health and Expressions of Sympathy

🎧 *Say each sentence.*

What's the matter?   Oh, no.

What's wrong?   I'm so sorry to hear that.

I'm really sorry to hear that.

Gee, that's too bad.

Pair Practice

Practice the conversation and vocabulary with a partner. Use your own words.

A: Hello?

B: Hi, _____? Where have you been? I haven't seen you for days.

A: Well, I've been sick _____.

B: Oh, no. _____?

A: _____.

B: _____. Hope you feel better soon.

A: _____.

☑ **Now you know how to ask about someone's absence and offer sympathy.**

In Your Own Words   **Look at the picture on page 49. With a partner, name the different ailments of the people in the picture.**

SOCIAL LANGUAGE AND GRAMMAR 2
How to suggest a course of action/express sympathy

Conversation

🎧 *Read and listen to the conversation.*

A: Hello?

B: Hi, Emma. This is Jan. How's it going?

A: So-so. I've had a terrible sore throat all day.

B: Gee, that's too bad. Have you tried chicken soup?

A: No. Will it help?

B: Absolutely. You'll feel better in no time.

🎧 *Listen again and practice.*

Vocabulary • Words That Describe How People Feel

🎧 *Look at the pictures. Say each word or phrase.*

so-so	**not great**	**bad**	**awful**	**terrible**	**horrible**

Pair Practice

Practice the conversation and vocabulary with a partner. Use your own words.

A: Hello?

B: Hi, _____. This is _____. How's it going?

A: _____. I've had _____.

B: _____. Have you tried _____?

A: No. Will it help?

B: Absolutely. You'll feel better in no time.

☑ **Now you know how to suggest a remedy when someone is sick.**

The Present Perfect—Form

Form the present perfect with **have** or **has** and a past participle.

past participle

I **haven't seen** you for days.

questions	possible answers
Have you tried a ginger ale and rice diet?	Yes, I have.
Have you ever **had** the flu?	No, I haven't. (*or* No, I never have.)

TIP: *Ever* means "in your entire life."

Use **how long** to ask about periods of time.

How long has he **been** in the hospital?

GRAMMAR TASK: Find a question in the present perfect in the photo story on pages 38–39. Answer it in your own words.

Grammar in a Context

Complete these conversations. Use the simple past tense or the present perfect and **for** or **since**.

Hello, Maria? This is Albert.

Albert? Is it really you? I _____ from you
1. hear / not
_____ last summer.
2.

I know, Maria. It's a long, long story.

How was your trip?

Great. We _____
3. spend
two weeks in Paris.

Were you in London?

Yes, but only _____
4.
two days.

I'm starved. I _____ _____ last night.
5. eat / not   **6.**

How come?

How long _____ you _____
7. have
that sore throat?

_____ two days. _____
8.   **9.**
the day before yesterday.

Vocabulary • Remedies

🎧 Look at the pictures. Say the name of each remedy.

ice   a hot water bottle   a heating pad   a hot shower   chicken soup   a pain killer   tea with milk and honey

Grammar and Vocabulary with a Partner

Practice the grammar and vocabulary with a partner.

A: Have you ever tried _____ for _____? (chicken soup / a cold)

B: Yes, I have. (*or* No, I haven't, *or* No, I never have.)

In Your Own Words

Look at the picture on page 49. With a partner, create a conversation for the woman talking to her friend on the cell phone. Use your own words.

In the Doctor's Office

Make your classroom a doctor's office. Some classmates are receptionists. The rest of the classmates are either doctors or patients.

*Patients, go to page 144.
Doctors, go to page 144.*

Receptionists, ask each patient the questions on this form. Fill in the form together. Then send each patient to see one of the doctors.

Work in groups of 3 – a receptionist, a doctor, a patient.

Pine Street Medical Group

Name: _____

Address: _____

Phone number: _____

Reason for this visit: _____

Have you been here before? _____

Have you had any operations? _____

Have you ever had any serious medical problems? _____

Receptive Model

Listening with a Purpose

Determine Context

🎧 *Listen to the conversation. Then answer these questions.*

1. Where is Ellen? _____

2. Who is sick? _____

Focus Attention

Read the following pairs of sentences.

1. ☐ Ellen is giving a kidney to her sister.

☐ Ellen has given a kidney to her sister.

2. ☐ Pat has been on dialysis for five years.

☐ Pat was on dialysis for five years.

3. ☐ Ellen will donate the kidney this morning.

☐ Ellen will donate the kidney tomorrow morning.

🎧 *Listen to the conversation again. Check the sentence in each pair that is true.*

Pronunciation
/n/, /ŋ/, and /m/

 *Read and listen to these words. Listen carefully to the final sound of each word.*

/n/	/ŋ/	/m/
sun	sung	some
ran	rang	Kim
thin	thing	ham
win	king	Pam
pan	wing	Sam

 *Listen again and repeat.*

Pronunciation Bongo

(reinforces /n/, /ŋ/, and /m/)

Complete the card with the fifteen words from the pronunciation list, but in your own order.

Choose a leader. The leader reads the words from the pronunciation list, writing down each word on a piece of paper.

Classmates circle each word on their cards as the leader reads them. The first classmate to circle four words in any direction calls out BONGO. That person is the next leader.

An Article from Pocket Digest

Before You Read: Think about some very serious health problems. How can they change your life?

Read the article. 🎧

Pocket Digest

Ron's Challenge

Ron Hammer loved basketball. One afternoon on his way to a basketball game, he was walking and dreaming about playing college basketball the following year.

At the same time as Ron was walking to the game, Sam Glen was walking to his car. Sam was feeling tired. He knew it was time to stop working so hard. Sam got into his car and headed home. He was driving down Seventh Avenue when he had a heart attack. Sam's car hit Ron so hard that Ron was thrown three feet into the air.

Ron woke up in a hospital room. When he learned that both his legs were broken, he realized his college basketball dreams were over. Ron did what the doctors told him, but his progress was slow. When he left the hospital, Ron was sent to a rehab center for physical therapy.

A week after he arrived there, he met Sunny Chen. Sunny was a former coach. His legs were paralyzed from a skiing accident. Even though he couldn't move his legs, Sunny coached a basketball team called the Suns. Everyone on the team played from a wheelchair. Sunny invited Ron to join the game. Ron played badly, but for the first time since the accident, he stopped feeling sorry for himself.

After becoming a part of the Suns, Ron improved quickly. Basketball was like medicine for him. And whenever Ron became depressed or angry, Sunny was there to encourage him and help him. The day before Ron left the center, he had dinner with Sunny. He asked Sunny how he managed to be so generous and cheerful, even with his paralysis.

Sunny smiled and said, "It's really quite simple. When you keep your face to the sun, the shadows fall behind."

Comprehension: Identifying the Main Idea

What is the most important thing we can learn from this story?

a. Sports can teach people about life.

b. Positive thoughts and actions can help people with their health problems.

c. Skiing can be dangerous.

Writing
A Get-Well Letter

Sam Glen, the man who had the heart attack that caused Ron's injury, did not die. But he is very sick and depressed and hasn't gone to work in a month. He knows that the accident injured Ron, and he feels very bad about that.

Ron is not angry at Sam. He wants to write a letter to Sam, telling him about his own condition.

Pretend you are Ron. Write a get-well letter to Sam Glen.

Dear Mr. Glen,

I heard that you haven't gone to work in a month. I'm sorry that you are feeling bad. I want you to know that I'm not angry. I am better

I think...

In my opinion...

because...

Talk with a partner. Compare your opinions.

Do all people react to medical problems in the same way? What are some reactions that people have when they are sick or have terrible accidents? Compare Sam and Ron. Remember Pat and Ellen from Listening with a Purpose on page 45.

I feel...

I don't think...

What about you?

Warm up: Talk about this picture with a partner.
• Where are the people? • Who are the people?
• Say something about each one. • What are their problems?

Then: Create conversations for the people. OR Tell a story.
Say as much as you can.

49

What do you think I should do?

Warm up: *Have you ever listened to a radio talk show? What did the people talk about? Read or listen.* 🎧

I'm Rhoda Molina, and this is "What's on Your Mind?" Our toll-free number is 1–800–777–0055.

Jeff from Portland, Oregon. What's on your mind?

Hi, Rhoda. I have a problem with my dad. I need some advice.

OK. What's the problem?

ON AIR

Well, he was an athlete when he was in school, and now he's trying to get <u>me</u> to be one.

And you don't want to?

Right. I like sports, but I'm really not into competition. And my dad wants me to be a star.

What do you think I should do?

Have you talked to your dad about this?

Comprehension: Understanding Meaning from Context

Circle the choice closer in meaning to each underlined phrase or sentence.

1. <u>What's on your mind</u>?

   a. What's your problem?   **b.** What's your opinion?

2. Why don't you just sit down and <u>level with your dad</u>?

   a. criticize your dad?   **b.** tell your dad the truth?

Comprehension: Interpretation and Analysis

Answer these questions.

1. Does Jeff have a good relationship with his father?

2. Do you think Jeff should do what his father wants?

HOW TO **ask for and give advice**

Should

Use **should** to give advice or make a strong suggestion.

> Jeff, you **should** talk to your dad.

Should doesn't have **-s** in the third-person singular. Use the base form of a verb after **should.**

> base form   base form
> Jeff **shouldn't complain** so much. He **should do** something.

GRAMMAR TASK: Find a sentence with **should** in the photo story on pages 50–51.

To make questions with **should,** place **should** before the subject of the sentence.

questions	possible answers
Should Rhoda help Jeff?	Yes, she should.
What **should** Jeff tell his dad?	The truth.
Shouldn't we call Rhoda, too?	Yes. Let's call her now.

GRAMMAR TASK: Answer the second question in your own words.

Grammar in a Context

In addition to doing her radio show, Rhoda Roberts writes a newspaper advice column.

Ask Rhoda

Dear Rhoda:

*Complete the letters in Rhoda's column with **should** or **shouldn't** and the indicated verbs.*

Dear Rhoda:

Here's my problem. My twenty-eight-year-old son has been living with me ever since he lost his job six months ago. The thing is, he won't look for a new job. He sleeps till noon every day. I tell him he _____ work, but he says I'm being too
1. look for

critical. What _____ I _____? Am I being too hard on him?
2. do

Frustrated in Florida

Dear Frustrated:

In my opinion, you aren't being too hard on him at all. A twenty-eight-year-old man _____ himself. And he certainly _____ till noon. Give him two weeks
3. support **4. sleep**

to find a job. If he doesn't, move his things out on the street.

****

Dear Rhoda:

I've got a problem. A girl I like in my science class asked me to lend her my lab workbook so she could copy my answers. _____ I _____ it, Rhoda? I
5. do

don't want to, but I'm afraid that if I don't give it to her she won't like me anymore.

Desperate in Denver

Dear Desperate:

Is your head on straight? Of course you _____ her your workbook. That's
6. give

cheating, and you could get into big trouble.

Grammar with a Partner

Talk about Rhoda's answers. Do you agree or disagree with them?

Conversation

🎧 *Read and listen to the conversation.*

A: What should I do? I'm going crazy.

B: Why? What's the matter?

A: I can't find my car keys.

B: Have you looked in your coat pocket?

A: Of course!

B: Well, try looking in the car.

A: Good idea.

🎧 *Listen again and practice.*

Vocabulary • Personal Items

🎧 *Look at the pictures. Say each word.*

a wallet   **a checkbook**   **keys**   **pills**   **(sun)glasses**   **a purse**   **a briefcase**

Vocabulary • Places and Things in the House

🎧 *Look at the pictures. Say the name of each place or thing.*

a bathroom   **a medicine cabinet**   **a refrigerator**   **a closet**   **a desk**

Pair Practice

Practice the conversation and vocabulary with a partner. Use your own words.

A: What should I do? I'm going crazy.

B: Why? What's the matter?

A: I can't find my _____.

B: Have you looked in _____?

A: _____!

B: Well, try looking in _____.

A: Good idea.

☑ **Now you know how to ask for advice. You also know how to give it.**

In Your Own Words Look at the pictures on page 61. With a partner, name all the things you see on Rhoda's desk.

SOCIAL LANGUAGE AND GRAMMAR 2

HOW TO suggest an alternative

Could
Use *could* to suggest alternatives or state possibilities.
We *could* go to the movies tonight. Or we *could* rent a video.
Could doesn't have *-s* in the third-person singular. Use the base form of a verb after *could*.
base form
We *could eat* out tonight.
Remember that the word *could* is also a past form of *can*. This *could* shows past ability.
Margaret *could* play the piano when she was five years old.
GRAMMAR TASK: Find a sentence with *could* in the photo story on pages 50-51.

Grammar in a Context

*Complete the conversations with **could** and the indicated verbs.*

Pam is failing English. Any ideas?

Well, you _____ with her for an
1. work
hour or so every night. That's what I did when Jim was failing math. Or you _____ her a tutor.
2. get

_____ from
3. we / not / drive
Centerville to Trent?

Well, I guess you _____ , but
4. drive
I don't recommend it. The road is pretty bad. I think you should fly.

In Your Own Words Look at the second picture on page 61. With a partner, create a conversation for Rhoda and the woman. The woman tells Rhoda her problem. Rhoda suggests alternatives. Use your own words.

☑ **Now you know how to suggest an alternative.**

Improvise

Look at this chart from a magazine. Check the items that are sometimes a problem in your life. Tell your partner about your problems. Then give each other advice about the problems.

My Life Is Driving Me Crazy!

Take this quiz. If you check more than three boxes, your life is driving you crazy. Get some advice quick. Make changes!

My parents (*or* my children) don't understand me. ☐

My neighbor's dog barks every night. ☐

My boyfriend (*or* my girlfriend, *etc.*) doesn't pay enough attention to me. ☐

My husband (*or* my wife, *etc.*) isn't home very often. ☐

I don't have enough money. ☐

No one understands me. ☐

I don't like my work (*or* my classes). ☐

I don't have enough time. ☐

My job is boring. ☐

Writing

A Letter to an Advice Column

Choose one of the problems from the chart, or choose some other problem. Write a letter to a classmate, asking for advice. Invent a name for yourself and sign your letter with it. Then exchange letters and write advice and suggestions to each other.

Dear Christine,

My life is driving me crazy. No one understands me. My boss says I don't do enough work, my husband complains about my cooking, and my children don't study. I don't know what to do.

Going Crazy in Goshen

Dear John,

I'm writing to ask your advice about a problem with Stan, my boyfriend. He's nice to me when the two of us are together. But when we go out with his friends, he ignores me. For example, last weekend we went to a restaurant and met some of his friends. For two hours he talked to them but not to me. What should I do?

Ignored in Indiana

Pronunciation

/ʊ/ and /u/

🎧 *Look at the pictures. Listen to the words and sentences.*

full
The glass is full.

fool
He's a fool.

soot
Look at the soot.

suit
Luke was wearing a white suit.

🎧 *Listen to the words.*

/ʊ/	full	soot	look
/u/	fool	suit	Luke

🎧 *Listen again and repeat.*

Sound Matches

(reinforces /ʊ/ and /u/)

Make a card for each of the six words. With a partner, take turns reading words to each other from the cards. Your partner holds up a card that matches the word you said. How many matches can you make on the first try?

full
fool

soot
suit

look
Luke

Reading

An Interview of a Sports Hero

Before You Read: Look at the photo story on pages 50–51 again. Talk about Jeff's problems. Think about whether his father is helping him to be an athlete. Then, when you read this interview, compare Karen's experience with Jeff's.

Read the interview. 🎧

Renfro: Good afternoon, everyone. I'm Tom Renfro. Today we're interviewing local athlete Karen Curtis, who as many of you know is a member of this year's Olympic diving team. Thanks for being with us, Karen.

Curtis: Thanks for having me, Tom.

Renfro: So Karen, how long have you been a diver?

Curtis: Well, let me see . . . a long time now . . . since I was six years old.

Renfro: How did you get started?

Curtis: Well, my parents died when I was young, and I lived with my grandparents. My grandfather was a diving coach, and he encouraged me.

Renfro: Hmm. Encouraged you, huh? That's nice to hear. We hear a lot today about adults pressuring kids to do things. Was it mainly his idea, or your idea?

Curtis: My idea, really. It was something I always wanted to do. He never actually told me I should dive.

Renfro: Well, tell me this: You were national champion last year, and everybody says you're a sports hero. What's the hardest part about being a famous athlete?

Curtis: Hmm. I'd say it's probably staying humble. Everybody is always saying you're great, and it's easy to start believing it. But there are a lot of great divers out there. Some days you're a little luckier, that's all.

Renfro: But you've worked very hard, haven't you? Don't you think you should win some kind of medal? From what I've heard, you're the favorite for the silver. And maybe you'll even win the gold, right?

Curtis: Well, if I do win a medal, great. If I don't, it's still an honor to be part of the Olympics. I just want to do my best for my country and my team.

Renfro: Well, Karen, that's a wonderful attitude. We wish you the best of luck.

Curtis: Thank you very much.

Comprehension: Confirming Content

*Mark the following statements **true**, **false**, or **I don't know**.*

	True	False	I don't know.
1. Karen has been a diver for six years.	☐	☐	☐
2. Karen lives with her parents.	☐	☐	☐
3. Karen has trained for the Olympics for four years.	☐	☐	☐
4. Karen thinks that luck is part of winning a medal.	☐	☐	☐
5. Karen's grandfather said Karen should be a diver.	☐	☐	☐

Bonus Question: Explain what Karen means when she says "staying humble."

Listening with a Purpose

Determine Context

🎧 *Listen to the editorial on a sports radio station. Choose a title that expresses its main idea.*

   a. "What Is Important in Sports?"

   b. "Injuries That Athletes Get"

Comprehension: Analysis of Point of View

🎧 *Listen again to the editorial. This time listen for the opinion of the speaker.*

*Mark the following statements **true** or **false**, according to your understanding of the speaker's point of view.*

	True	False
1. Winning should be everything.	☐	☐
2. Money has been a good influence on sports.	☐	☐
3. Ken's parents have a bad attitude about sports.	☐	☐
4. It was good that Kerri competed.	☐	☐
5. It is important to concentrate on how we play, not only on winning.	☐	☐

Heart to Heart

Talk to a partner about these questions. Compare your opinions. Give examples.

Should parents make their children play sports (*or* choose a certain career *or* play a musical instrument)?

What is the difference between parents' pressuring their children to do something and encouraging them to do something?

 Olympic Mania

(reinforces wh- questions and answers)

Divide into groups of four. First try to answer the questions together. Then play the game.

Partners B, C, and D, turn to page 145.
Partner A, ask the questions.
Partners B, C, and D, give the answers on page 145.

Partner A, for each question, two partners will give the correct answer. One partner will give an incorrect answer. Write the correct answer.

Question	Correct Answer
1. Where were the ancient Olympics?	
2. How long have we held the modern Olympics?	
3. Which country won the most medals in the 1996 Olympics?	
4. Which of these is <u>not</u> an official summer Olympic sport? (American football / boxing)	
5. Which of these is <u>not</u> an official winter Olympic sport? (cross-country skiing / baseball)	
6. Which two countries participated in the 1980 Olympics in Moscow? (China / the Soviet Union / the U.S.A.)	
7. Nadia Comaneci was the first gymnast to win a perfect 10 in the Olympics. What country was she from?	
8. How many countries participated in the 1996 Olympics? (197 / 302)	

Warm up: Talk about the two pictures with a partner.
• What time is it in each picture? • Talk about the people.
• What problems do they have?

Then: Create conversations for the people. OR Tell a story.
Say as much as you can.

Review, SelfTest, and Extra Practice

Part 1

Review

I Haven't Seen You All Day!

Rick and Tim are two students. They are roommates. Tim works for Professor Berg in the biology lab.

🎧 *Listen to the conversation between Rick and Tim.*

SelfTest

Grammar: Verb Form Review

Now read Rick and Tim's conversation. Choose the correct item to complete each blank.

Rick: Hey, where have you _____? I haven't seen you all day!
　　　　　　　　　　　　　　　1. being / been

Tim: In the lab. I _____ Professor Berg set up the lab experiments. Why?
　　　　　　　　2. was helping / helping

Rick: Well, some woman _____ twice—something about a visa. She wants

  3. was calling / called

you to call her back.

Tim: What's her name?

Rick: Uh. . . Ms. Ikeda, I think. Her number's by the phone. . . . What's all this

about a visa?

Tim: I _____ to Brazil in that summer exchange program. Remember?

  4. 'm going / go

Rick: Oh, yeah. Right.

****

Tim: Hello, may I speak with Ms. Ikeda?

Ms. Ikeda: This is Nancy Ikeda. May I help you?

Tim: Ms. Ikeda, this is Tim Sharp. I _____ your call.

  5. 'm returning / return

Ms. Ikeda: Oh, yes, Mr. Sharp. I _____ your application here, but we need to

  6. was having / have

see your passport to issue you a visa.

Tim: Oh. OK. What _____ your hours?

  7. were / are

Ms. Ikeda: We're open from 10 A.M. to 4 P.M. We _____ in the Federal

  8. were / 're

Building on Tenth Avenue. Ninth floor.

Tim: OK, Ms. Ikeda. I _____ there tomorrow afternoon.

  9. 'm / 'll be

Pair Practice

🎧 *Listen again to part of Rick and Tim's conversation. Write what you hear in the blanks.*

A: Hey, where _____? I haven't seen you _____!

B: _____. I was _____. Why?

A: Well, _____.

Now work with a partner. Use your own words in the blanks.

Part 2

Review

This Is the Ugliest Color I've Ever Seen!

🎧 *Read or listen to the conversation in the luggage department of a store.*

Helen: Good afternoon, sir. May I help you?

Man: I doubt it, but we'll see. I need to exchange this suitcase. I bought it last week, and I don't mind telling you that the man who sold it to me was the worst salesperson I've ever met.

Helen: I'm sorry to hear that, sir. What's the problem with this suitcase? Hmm. I didn't know we sold this brand here at our store.

Man: Well, for one thing, it turns out that it's too small. I need something bigger. For another, I've decided it's the ugliest color I've ever seen! It makes me sick.

Helen: All right, sir. Let's take a look at the luggage over here. We have a wide variety of suitcases. This is a nice one.

Man: No, no, that's too big. I need something smaller. What about this leather suitcase?

Helen: Well, sir, that's our most expensive brand. I'd recommend this suitcase here. It's a lot cheaper. It's not a famous brand, but it's about the same quality as the leather one. Definitely a better buy for your money.

Man: What? Who do you think I am? Do I look like somebody who can't afford to buy any suitcase I want?

Helen: No, sir. I was just thinking about saving you some money. The leather suitcase costs more.

Man: How long have you worked here?

Helen: Well, since last March. Why?

Man: Are you Helen Townsend?

Helen: Well, yes, sir, I am, but...

Man: Would you like to come and work for me, Ms. Townsend?

Helen: Excuse me? I don't understand, sir.

Man: I'm sorry I was rude. I'm Stan Webber from The Wrap. You submitted an application to my company. In your application letter, you invited employers to come to the luggage department at Bloom's and pretend to be interested in luggage. Well, I did. You're the nicest salesperson I've ever met. Do you want the job?

SelfTest

Comprehension: Confirming Content, Drawing Conclusions

 Read or listen to the conversation again. Then mark the following statements ***true, false,*** *or* ***I don't know.***

	True	False	I don't know.
1. The man is really a customer.	☐	☐	☐
2. The man actually bought the suitcase at this store.	☐	☐	☐
3. The man says the color of the suitcase is ugly.	☐	☐	☐
4. Helen wanted the man to buy the store's most expensive suitcase.	☐	☐	☐
5. The man is a boss in another company.	☐	☐	☐

Improvise

Work with a partner. Improvise a conversation between a difficult customer and a salesperson. The customer wants to exchange an item in a store.

Extra Practice

Part 3

Review

Nice to Meet You.

 Listen to the conversation.

Comprehension: Focus Attention

Read the following incomplete statements.

1. The two people are on _____.

   a. an elevator   **b.** a bus

2. They are both going _____.

   a. to work   **b.** to the passport office

3. Their names are _____.

   a. Kristin and Tom   **b.** Karen and Tim

4. They have been here for _____.

   a. about ten minutes   **b.** half an hour

5. The man has to start work at _____.

   a. ten o'clock   **b.** four o'clock

 Listen to the conversation again and complete the statements.

Extra Practice

Improvise

With a partner, improvise a conversation on an elevator that gets stuck in one of the following places.

   1. an office building

   2. a large store

Part 4

Review

I Just Don't Think I Can Come in Today.

Read more about Helen Townsend.

    Last year, Helen Townsend was working in the luggage department at Bloom's Department Store. Helen was looking for a better job. In an application letter, she asked employers to come to the luggage department at Bloom's and pretend to be interested in luggage. Stan Webber, the owner of a women's clothing store, The Wrap, actually did this. He thought Helen was an excellent salesperson. He gave her a job in his company.

Helen has worked for Stan for several months. Today, though, she's feeling very sick. Early this morning she called Stan to tell him she couldn't come to work.

SelfTest

Social Language

Read this conversation between Helen and Stan. Complete the conversation by choosing the correct item in each case.

Improvise

Work with a partner. Improvise a telephone conversation between a boss and an employee. The employee is sick and cannot come to work. The boss suggests a remedy.

Part 5

Review

Did You Know . . . ?

🎧 *Listen to the radio quiz show.*

SelfTest

Grammar: The Comparative and Superlative Forms of Adjectives

Learn some interesting facts. Complete the sentences with the comparative or superlative forms of the adjectives.

1. (long) _____ _____ river in the United States is the Missouri.

2. (far) Of these three countries—Japan, Ukraine, and Norway—Norway is _____ _____ north.

3. (populated) China is _____

_____ _____ country in the world.

4. (expensive) It is _____ _____ to live in New York City than it is to live in Dublin.

5. (bad) _____ _____ accident at a nuclear power plant happened at Chernobyl.

6. (large) _____ _____ country in area in the world is Russia.

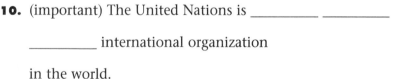

7. (fast) _____ _____ land animal is the cheetah.

8. (dangerous) A cobra is _____ _____ than a rattlesnake.

9. (good) The movie *The English Patient* was _____ _____ picture in 1996, according to the Academy Awards.

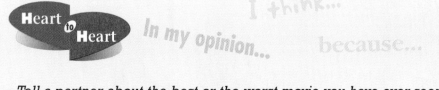

10. (important) The United Nations is _____ _____ _____ international organization in the world.

Heart to Heart

I think...   *In my opinion...*   *because...*

Tell a partner about the best or the worst movie you have ever seen. Compare your opinions.

I feel...   *I don't think...*   *What about you?*

Extra Practice

Review

Would You Like to Have Coffee?

Read the conversation between Karen Curtis and Tim Sharp.

Comprehension: Drawing Conclusions

Read Karen and Tim's conversation again. Then choose the phrase that best completes the following statement.

Karen doesn't know if she should go to Venezuela. She is afraid that _____ when she's out of the country.

   a. her grandfather will be angry

   b. her grandfather will get sick

   c. her grandfather will miss her

Heart to Heart

I think...

In my opinion...

because...

What do you think Karen should (or could) do? Talk about it with a partner. Use should and could. Then create an ending for the story. Tell your ending to the class. The class decides which endings they like the best.

I feel...

I don't think...

What about you?

Extra Practice

◢ SOCIAL LANGUAGE SelfTest

Circle the appropriate statement or question to complete each of the following conversations.

1. A: I don't know if you remember me. We were in the same English class last year.

   B: _____

     a. I was taking a shower when the phone rang.

     b. I took an English class last semester.

     c. Well, I don't really want to.

     d. Sure I do. You were always telling jokes.

2. A: How's it going?

   B: _____

     a. Not too well.

     b. Not really.

     c. I never go anywhere.

     d. I'm going on vacation next month.

3. A: _____

    B: Sure. How about tomorrow?

        a. When are you going to be back?

        b. Would you like to have lunch sometime?

        c. Do you like Italian food?

        d. Are you going to be home tonight?

4. A: I was wondering—could you do me a favor?

    B. _____

        a. Sure. How about Tuesday?

        b. Sure I do.

        c. Sure. What's up?

        d. Not too well.

5. A: My son won't eat vegetables. It's really a problem.

    B: _____

        a. Sure. I like vegetables.

        b. Try corn. Most kids like it.

        c. I'd be glad to.

        d. What's up?

6. A: How can I help you?

    B: _____

        a. I need to exchange this shirt. It's too small.

        b. Yes, please. I'd like to try it on.

        c. I don't like leather jackets.

        d. I'll take both of them.

7. A: _____

    B: Yes, please.

        a. What size do you wear?

        b. Do you work here?

        c. Where is the shoe department?

        d. Would you like to see them in another size?

8. A: I've had a terrible cough all week.

B: _____

    a. I'm sorry to hear that.

    b. How long have you had a cough?

    c. I'm glad to hear that.

    d. I haven't seen him for days.

9. A: Where have you been? I haven't seen you since Tuesday!

B: _____

    a. I haven't been to London, but I have been to Paris.

    b. Why not?

    c. Have you tried a rice diet?

    d. I've been sick in bed.

10. A: I've got a terrible stomachache!

B: _____

    a. Really? I've been sick all week.

    b. Where have you been?

    c. Gee, I'm sorry. Have you tried ginger ale?

    d. My stomach is bothering me.

11. A: _____

B: Well, you could apologize.

    a. What do you think I should do?

    b. What do you think will happen?

    c. Should I invite Ben to the party?

    d. Should I ask Mary about it?

12. A: Should I marry him?

B: _____

    a. Do you love him?

    b. That's not true.

    c. Well, I don't agree.

    d. I've never been married.

Aren't you Dick's brother-in-law?

Warm up: *These people are in an elevator. What do you talk about in an elevator? Read or listen.* 🎧

Oh hi, Lena. Could you hit ten?

No problem.

Boy, hasn't this weather been awful?

It sure has. Four rainy days in a row.

Hold the elevator, please.

Sure. Where are you going?

Seven, thank you.

Uh . . . You look familiar. Aren't you Dick Morgan's brother-in-law Jack?

Yes, I am.

I thought so.

Didn't you write that book about monkeys?

Mmm-hmm.

Comprehension: Confirming Content

*Mark the following statements **true**, **false**, or **I don't know.***

	True	False	I don't know.
1. The weather has been bad.	☐	☐	☐
2. Lena knew something about Jack before today.	☐	☐	☐
3. Jack has written several books.	☐	☐	☐

Comprehension: Interpretation and Analysis

Is Lena too friendly? Is Jack unfriendly? What do you think of their behavior?

HOW TO **make small talk/suggest future actions**

Conversation

🎧 *Read and listen to the conversation.*

> **A:** Hold the elevator, please. Thanks. Oh hi, Seth.
> **B:** Hi. Long time no see. How are you doing?
> **A:** Pretty good. Isn't this weather awful?
> **B:** Unbelievable.
> **A:** Well, this is my floor. Have a nice day.
> **B:** Thanks. You too.

🎧 *Listen again and practice.*

Vocabulary • Adjectives to Describe the Weather

🎧 *Look at the pictures. Say each adjective.*

good weather	
beautiful great fantastic gorgeous unbelievable	

bad weather	
awful terrible horrible unbelievable	

Pair Practice

Practice the conversation and vocabulary with a partner. Use your own words.

A: Hold the elevator, please. Thanks. Oh hi, _____.

B: Hi. Long time no see. How are you doing?

A: _____. Isn't this weather _____?

B: _____.

A: Well, this is my floor. Have a nice day.

B: Thanks. You too.

☑ **Now you know how to make small talk.**

Negative Questions

Use negative **yes-no** questions to ask about something you already think is true.

Aren't you Dick Morgan's brother-in-law? (The speaker thinks you are.)

Use negative **yes-no** questions to express an opinion you are sure others agree with.

Isn't this weather awful?

GRAMMAR TASK: Find other negative **yes-no** questions in the photo story on pages 74–75.

Grammar i.. a Context

*Complete the negative **yes-no** question in each conversation.*

Speech bubble: _____ you _____ a yellow
1. wear / not
blouse a few minutes ago?

Speech bubble: No, I wasn't. That was my twin sister, Robin.

Speech bubble: Where were you?

Speech bubble: No. We said four o'clock.

Speech bubble: _____ we _____
2. say / not
we were going to meet at four-thirty?

Speech bubble: Oh yeah. Sorry.

Speech bubble: _____ we _____ before?
3. meet / not

Speech bubble: Maybe we have. You look really familiar.

Speech bubble: _____ that
4. Be / not
Ron Stram?

Speech bubble: I don't know. But it sure looks like him.

Speech bubble: _____ her baby gorgeous?
5. Be / not

Speech bubble: Absolutely beautiful!

Why in Negative Questions

You can use **why** in negative questions to suggest future actions.

> **A:** **Why don't** we **go** to that concert together?
>
> **B:** Good idea.

GRAMMAR TASK: Change A's suggestion and B's response. Use your own words.

Grammar in a Context

Circle the appropriate response to each of the following statements.

1. A: That sure looks like Tom Hanks.

   B: Why don't we ask him for his autograph?

   B: Why don't we know him?

2. A: What beautiful weather!

   B: Why don't we like it?

   B: Why don't we go to the beach?

3. A: I'm so hungry I could eat a horse.

   B: Why don't you like horses?

   B: Why don't we eat lunch early?

Grammar with a Partner

*Walk around the room. Take turns making statements and suggesting future actions, using negative questions with **why**.*

Example: **A:** There's no class tomorrow.

            B: Why don't we go biking?

☑ **Now you know how to suggest future actions.**

In Your Own Words

Look at the picture on page 85. Make a suggestion that begins with *why*. Use your own words.

HOW TO **confirm identity/name family relationships**

Conversation

🎧 *Read and listen to the conversation.*

A: Aren't you Diane's sister-in-law?
B: Yes, I am.
A: I thought so. By the way, I'm Peter Tanaka.
B: Nice to meet you, Peter. My name's Gloria Harris.

🎧 *Listen again and practice.*

Vocabulary • **Family Relationships**

🎧 *Look at the family tree. Say the name of each relationship.*

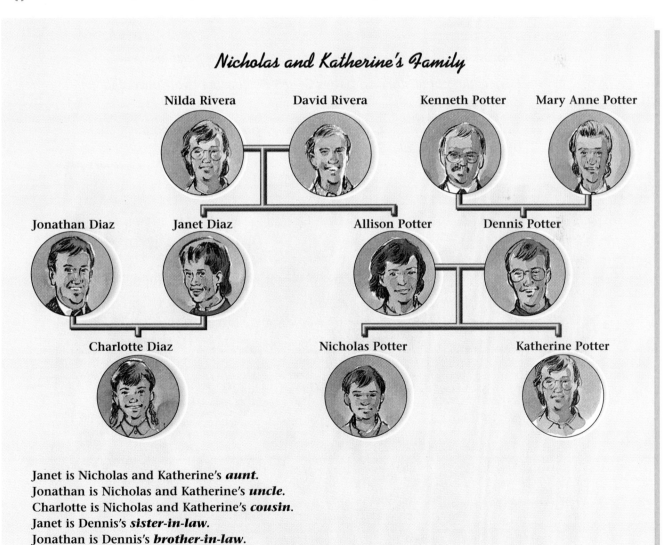

Nicholas and Katherine's Family

Nilda Rivera   David Rivera   Kenneth Potter   Mary Anne Potter

Jonathan Diaz   Janet Diaz   Allison Potter   Dennis Potter

Charlotte Diaz   Nicholas Potter   Katherine Potter

Janet is Nicholas and Katherine's **aunt**.
Jonathan is Nicholas and Katherine's **uncle**.
Charlotte is Nicholas and Katherine's **cousin**.
Janet is Dennis's **sister-in-law**.
Jonathan is Dennis's **brother-in-law**.
Kenneth and Mary Anne are Allison's **in-laws** (**father-in-law** and **mother-in-law**).

Practice the conversation and vocabulary with a partner. Use your own words.

A: Aren't you _____'s _____?

B: Yes, I am.

A: I thought so. By the way, I'm _____.

B: Nice to meet you, _____. My name's _____.

☑ **Now you know how to confirm someone's identity and name more family relationships.**

Improvise

Improvise a scene in an elevator with one or more partners.

Review the photo story on pages 74–75. Review the two Conversations on pages 76 and 79.

Talk about the weather, ask each other to press buttons, confirm each other's identities, etc. Say as much as you can.

Reading

An Article from a Psychology Magazine

Before You Read: When you want something, do you usually ask for it? Why or why not? Read the article. 🎧

═══ Psychology Tomorrow ═══

Understanding Small Talk

Madeleine McGowan, Ph.D.

A week before Andrea's twenty-ninth birthday, her husband, Greg, asked her what she wanted for her birthday. She told him not to get her anything. On the day of her birthday, Andrea was very unhappy when Greg had nothing for her. Greg was confused. He said, "You told me not to buy you a gift." She replied, "I know. But you didn't have to listen to me."

What happened? Didn't Andrea say what she meant? Maybe not, because as it turns out, Andrea really did want a gift. So why didn't she say so? And how can Greg understand Andrea's behavior? A good start for him might be to read a book by linguist Deborah Tannen.

Linguists study how languages work.

Some study the history and grammar of languages. Others, like Tannen, study how people use language in their everyday lives. She analyzes hundreds of conversations in homes, at work, in coffee shops, on elevators, at supermarkets. She explores the differences between the way men and women speak and the way people from different geographic areas speak.

Deborah Tannen can help us understand the messages behind words. Her books can help us understand why our conversation flows with some people and dies with others.

Such understanding can help us in our social as well as business relationships.

Comprehension: Factual Recall

Complete each sentence by circling the correct letter.

1. Andrea told Greg _____.

   a. to buy her an inexpensive gift   **b.** not to buy her a gift

2. Some linguists study _____.

   a. the history and grammar of languages   **b.** homes, work, coffee shops, elevators, and supermarkets

3. Deborah Tannen is a linguist who studies _____.

   a. the history and grammar of languages   **b.** everyday conversations

4. Tannen helps people understand the differences between the way _____.

   a. men and women travel to different geographical areas   **b.** men and women communicate

Heart to Heart In my opinion... I think... because...

Talk with a partner. Compare your opinions.

Do men and women have different conversation styles? In what ways?

Do people in different places have different conversation styles? Explain.

I feel... I don't think... What about you?

Pronunciation

/t/ and /θ/

🎧 *Listen and then repeat the names of these streets and avenues.*

Bath Street	Tin Street	Tenth Avenue	Threeway Avenue
Bat Street	Thin Street	Tent Avenue	Treeway Avenue

 # Watch Your Pronunciation!

(reinforces /t/ and /θ/)

Partner A, look at this map.

Partner B, your map is on page 145.

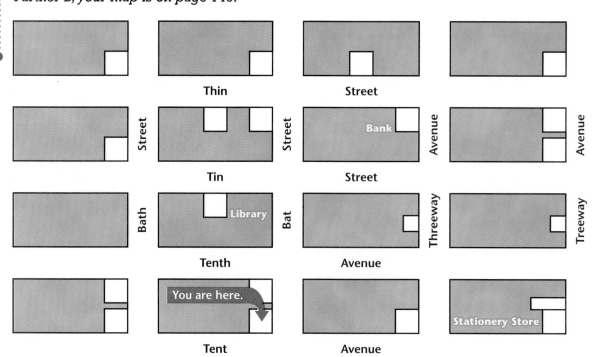

Partner A, you want to know where the following places are:

the drugstore
the supermarket
the movie theater

When you find out, mark the places on your map.

Example:

A: Excuse me. Could you tell me where the nearest _____ is?

B: Yes. It's on the corner of _____ and _____.

OR

Yes. It's on _____ between _____ and _____.

Receptive Model

Listening with a Purpose

Determine Context

Listen to the conversation. Then listen again and circle the correct letter.

1. Who are the two main speakers?

   a. a gas station attendant and a woman   **b.** a couple

2. Where are they going?

   a. to the movies   **b.** to Treeway Avenue

3. What happens?

   a. The woman gets directions in a gas station.   **b.** The man gets directions in a gas station.

Focus Attention

*Listen to the conversation again. This time listen for suggestions that begin with **why**. Write them here in the box.*

female speaker	male speaker

Writing

An Invitation to a Party

Read the invitation. Either write or e-mail Marie, telling her why you can't come.

You're Invited

Occasion: __Kim's Birthday__

Date: __March 13__

Time: __6:30 P.M.__

Place: __44 Devoe Road__

Directions: __Take the no. 5 bus to the corner of Devoe and King Street. We're the second house on the right. Please arrive on time. This is a surprise party!__

Regrets Only: __Marie Salinger 238-1722 or e-mail Maries@dr.com__

Now complete this invitation. Write directions to the party from your school. Give directions by car, by bus, and/or by train.

You're Invited

Occasion: _____

Date: _____

Time: _____

Place: _____

Directions: _____

_____

_____

_____

Regrets Only: _____

Talk about this picture with a partner.
- Who are the people? • What is the weather like?
- Where are the people? • Where are they going?
- Are they having problems? • What should they do?

Create conversations for the people. OR Tell a story.
Say as much as you can.

85

We'd better find a gas station—fast!

Warm up: Look at the pictures in order. What do you think is happening? Listen.

Comprehension: Inference and Interpretation

🎧 *Listen again to "We'd better find a gas station—fast!" Complete each sentence by circling the correct letter.*

1. The family is _____.

   a. driving to work   **b.** on vacation   **c.** driving to school

2. There are bathrooms in _____.

   a. the trunk   **b.** vans   **c.** gas stations

3. The most important problem is _____.

   a. the bathroom   **b.** the motel   **c.** the flat tire

Comprehension: Understanding Meaning from Context

🎧 *Listen again. Find these items in the pictures.*

a tire	a flat tire	a spare tire	a front seat	a back seat	a seat belt
a jack	a road	a speed limit sign	a speedometer	a steering wheel	a gas gauge

HOW **TO describe quantities/request and offer service**

Vocabulary • Words and Phrases That Tell "How Many" and "How Much"

🎧 *Look at the pictures. Say each phrase.*

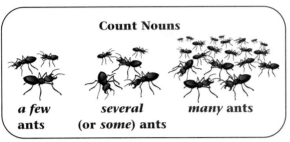

Count Nouns

a few ants   *several* (or *some*) ants   *many* ants

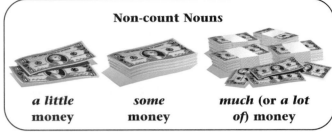

Non-count Nouns

a little money   *some* money   *much* (or *a lot of*) money

Count and Non-count Nouns

 *some* books and *some* money

 *a lot of* books and *a lot of* money

Quantifiers

Use *some* with both count and non-count nouns.

    We bought *some books*.   We're having *some trouble* with our car.

Remember that *some* is used in affirmative sentences and *any* in negative sentences.

    I have *some* time, but I don't have *any* money.

Both *some* and *any* are used in questions.

    Do you have *some* time today?   Do you have *any* time today?

Much is used in questions and negatives.

    Do you have *much* experience?   This car doesn't use *much* gas.

We usually use *a lot (of)* instead of *much* in affirmative sentences.

    My teacher gives *a lot of* homework.

Grammar in a Context

Complete the conversation by choosing the correct quantifier.

Mr. Appleby: Looks like you're having _____ car trouble.
                                     1. some / several

Mr. Hardy: Yes, we've got a flat tire and no spare. And we don't have _____ gas,
                                                           2. many / much

                either. We need to get to the nearest town.

Brad: Maybe we could hitchhike to town, Dad.

Mr. Appleby: Well, son, there aren't _____ cars on this road, and the gas stations
3. many / much

are all closed by now. The other thing is that it's going to be dark in

_____ minutes, and there aren't _____ motels around here.
4. a few / a little   **5.** some / any

Mr. Hardy: Oh, no. What now?

Mr. Appleby: Tell you what, folks. You could spend the night at our house. The kids

have all moved away, and we've got _____ extra beds. My wife
6. a little / a lot of

will be glad to have guests.

Mrs. Hardy: *(aside, to Mr. Hardy only):* Are you sure we should go with him?

After all, we don't even know him.

Mr. Hardy: *(to Mr. Appleby):* That's really nice of you. But we don't want to impose

on you.

Mr. Appleby: It's no trouble. . . . By the way, my name's John Appleby.

Mr. Hardy: Glad to meet you, Mr. Appleby. I'm Fred Hardy, and this is Patty. And

these are the kids: Maddie, Teddy, Heather, and Brad.

Mr. Appleby: Glad to meet you all. My wife and I have to do _____ shopping tomorrow
7. several / some

morning. We'll drive you to town then. . . . Now, let's see. . . . _____
8. Some / Much

of you can get in the cab here, and the rest of you can ride in the back.

☑ **Now you know how to describe quantities.**

Conversation

🎧 *Read and listen to the conversation.*

A: Can I help you?

B: Yes. Fill it up with premium, please.

A: Sure thing. Would you like me to check the oil?

B: Please. And could you check the tires, too?

A: Sure. Be glad to.

🎧 *Listen again and practice.*

Vocabulary • At the Gas Station

🎧 *Look at the pictures. Say each word or phrase.*

grades of gasoline

TOTAL SALE   GALLONS

PRICE PER GALLON

regular

medium

premium

services at a gas station

wash the windshield

check the oil

check the tires

Pair Practice

Practice the conversation and vocabulary with a partner. Use your own words.

A: Can I help you?

B: Yes. Fill it up with _____, please.

A: _____. Would you like me to _____?

B: Please. And could you _____, too?

A: Sure. Be glad to.

☑ **Now you know how to request services in a gas station.**

Pronunciation

/ð/ and /d/

 *Read and listen to these words.*

/ð/	/d/	/ð/	/d/

they   **day**

breathe   **breed**

 *Listen again and repeat.*

 *Now listen and circle the word you hear.*

1. they   day

2. breathe   breed

Minimal Pair Rummy

(reinforces /ð/ and /d/)

Form teams of two people each. Each person makes four cards, one for each word. One partner says one of the words and puts that card face down. His or her partner holds up the card with the same word. If the words match, the team gets a point.

Listening with a Purpose

Focus Attention

First read the following questions.

1. How long has Brad had a driver's license? _____

2. How old is Brad? _____

3. What is the speed limit on this road? _____

4. How fast was Brad going? _____

 *Now listen to the conversation in order to find the answers to the questions.*

TIP: Listen for numbers in the conversation.

 **Look at the second picture on page 97. With a partner, talk about this road. What's happening? What's the problem? Use your own words.**

How to **warn someone**

Had Better

Use **had better** and a base form to make a warning or a strong suggestion.

> **You'd better** get up! You're going to be late to work.

Had better does not have **-s** in the third-person singular. It is not followed by **to.**

> Your son **had better** study harder.

To form the negative of **had better,** place **not** after it.

> We**'d better not** go out tonight. The kids are sick.

Conversation

🎧 *Read and listen to the conversation.*

A: Uh-oh! You'd better slow down.

B: Why?

A: There's a police car up ahead.

B: Where?

A: About 200 yards up, on the right. Don't you see it?

B: Oh. Yeah.

🎧 *Listen again and practice.*

Vocabulary • On the Highway

🎧 *Look at the pictures. Say the name of each thing.*

a police car

a tow truck

an ambulance

a pickup truck

a truck

a van

a station wagon

an accident

a traffic jam

Pair Practice

Practice the conversation and vocabulary with a partner. Use your own words.

A: Uh-oh! You'd better slow down.

B: Why?

A: There's _____ up ahead.

B: Where?

A: About _____, on the _____. Don't you see it?

B: Oh. Yeah.

☑ **Now you know how to warn someone about a danger on the road.**

With a partner, look at the first picture on page 97. Create a conversation for the man and the woman. Use your own words.

Reading

An Excerpt from a Magazine Article

Before You Read: Think about age and driving.

Read the magazine article. 🎧

Too Young to Drive?

How important is a driver's license? In the U.S. it is very important. In most places, it is necessary to drive to get to work, to school, and to most social activities. Almost all large cities have public transportation systems, but even in those cities a lot of people have cars and use them often. Because cars are so necessary for independence, young people in the U.S. see a driver's license as a sign of being grown up. Getting a license means that you are an adult, with many of the privileges of adults.

How old should a person be to get a driver's license? Compared to many other countries, the minimum driving age in the U.S. is low. In 38 out of the 50 states, a person can get a driver's license at the age of 16. And in some states, the age is even lower. In Hawaii and Mississippi, for example, you can get a license at age 15. And in Louisiana, Montana, and New Mexico, you can get a license at 15 if

you've taken an approved driving course.

Some people in the U.S. think the driving age is too low, and they want to raise it. They say a person should be at least 18 to drive. After all, they argue, a car is a dangerous weapon that can kill people, and people younger than 18 often aren't very responsible. They note that drivers in the 16–24 age group have the most accidents.

Other people think the driving age is fine as it is. They believe that teenagers drive just as well as older people. Besides, they say, many teenagers have jobs, so they need to drive. Understandably, most young people don't want the driving age to change.

This is the way things are in the U.S., but what about the rest of the world? *U.S. Culture and Trends* is conducting a worldwide study. The results will appear in our next issue.

Comprehension: Understanding Meaning from Context

Circle the choice closest in meaning to each underlined word or phrase.

1. Young people in the U.S. see a driver's license as a sign of being <u>grown up</u>.

   a. tall   **b.** important   **c.** an adult

2. Compared to many other countries, the <u>minimum</u> driving age in the U.S. is low.

   a. lowest possible   **b.** best possible   **c.** highest possible

3. Some people in the U.S. think the driving age is too low, and they want to <u>raise it</u>.

   a. make it lower   **b.** make it higher   **c.** leave it the same

Writing

An E-Mail Message to the Editor of a Magazine

U.S. Culture and Trends *is conducting a worldwide study of people's opinions of the driving age. The study asks the following questions:*

> *What is the minimum driving age in your country?*
> *Is the minimum driving age too high or too low?*
> *Should the minimum driving age be the same all over the world?*

*Send an e-mail message to the editor of **U.S. Culture and Trends**. Express your opinion about the driving age. Look at the model and then compose your own e-mail message in the place provided on page 96.*

Example:

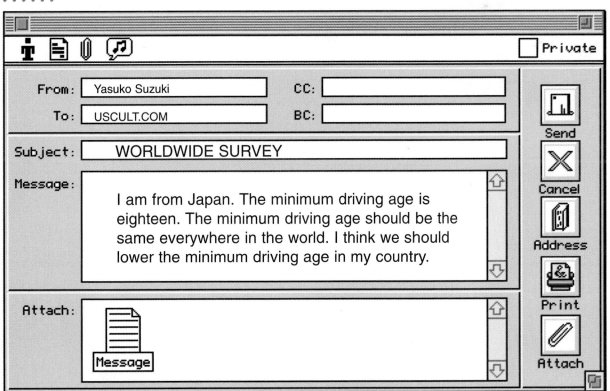

From: Yasuko Suzuki
To: USCULT.COM
CC:
BC:

Subject: WORLDWIDE SURVEY

Message:
I am from Japan. The minimum driving age is eighteen. The minimum driving age should be the same everywhere in the world. I think we should lower the minimum driving age in my country.

Attach: Message

Private | Send | Cancel | Address | Print | Attach

From: _____   CC: _____
To: _____   BC: _____

Subject: _____

Message:

Attach: [Message]

Send
Cancel
Address
Print
Attach

Private

Heart to Heart

I think...
In my opinion...   *because...*

Discuss these questions with a partner.
Compare your opinions.

Are young people better drivers than older people?

Are teenagers good drivers or bad drivers?

I feel...
I don't think...
What about you?

Improvise

Troubles on the Road

Listen to the story on pages 86–87 again. Listen to the Listening with a Purpose conversation again.

Write as many problems as you can. Then improvise a car trip with your partner. Have problems. Warn your partner of trouble on the road, stop for gas, ask for service, etc.

*W*arm up: Talk about these pictures with a partner.
• Where are the people? • Where are they going? • What
things are in the pictures? • What happens?

*T*hen: Create conversations for the man and the woman. OR
Tell the story of their date. Say as much as you can.

I'd like to make a reservation.

Receptive Model

Warm up: What's your favorite vacation place?
Read or listen. 🎧

How about a few days in San Diego?

Sounds great. But I'd rather go to San Francisco.

OK. But do you think we can?

Well, we're both off on Monday. If we take off Tuesday and Wednesday, we'll have five days off.

Uh-huh.

And if we use our frequent flier mileage, our flight to San Francisco will be free. The Royal Plaza's pretty reasonable. . . . So shall we go?

Why not?

Thank you for calling the Royal Plaza. This is Barbara speaking. Can I help you?

Yes, I'd like to make a reservation.

One moment. Please hold.

Comprehension: Understanding Meaning from Context

Find the following words and phrases in the photo story.
Then match each one with its meaning.

1. frequent flier mileage   not too expensive

2. reasonable   Do it.

3. Go for it.   room for two people

4. double   free airplane travel

How to make a reservation

The Real Conditional

Look at this sentence about the future.

present tense *future tense*

If you **give** me your name and credit card number, I'**ll hold** the room for you.

If we **don't ask** for a nonsmoking room, we **won't get** one.

Don't use the future tense after **if**.

GRAMMAR TASK: Look at the sentence with **if** in the third picture of the photo story. What are the tenses of the verbs?

Grammar in a Context

Complete the conversation with a present or future tense verb. Use contractions when possible.

Travel Agent: Here are your tickets and your itinerary. OK. You're all set.

Customer: Thanks. I've just got a couple of questions.

Travel Agent: Go ahead.

Customer: What if our plane _____ late
1. be
and we _____ to the hotel
2. get / not
until after midnight? _____
they _____ our room for us?
3. hold

Travel Agent: Of course, and someone _____
4. be
at the reservations desk all night.

Customer: Good. Now, say we don't like our room. What can we do?

Travel Agent: If there _____ another empty
5. be
room at those rates, the hotel _____ you have it.
6. let

Customer: I know this sounds ridiculous, but if we _____ our plane tickets,
7. lose

_____ we _____ any protection?
8. have

Travel Agent: Don't worry. Just call the airline. Someone there _____ you.
9. help

Customer: One final question. If we _____ return early, _____ we
10. have to

_____ a refund?
11. get

Travel Agent: No, I'm afraid not. In that case, there's nothing we can do.

Conversation

🎧 *Read and listen to the conversation.*

A: King Hotel. Claire speaking. How may I help you?

B: Do you have a double room available on October 14?

A: Smoking or nonsmoking?

B: Nonsmoking, please.

A: Let me check. Yes, we do. Shall I hold it for you?

B: Yes, please.

🎧 *Listen again and practice.*

Vocabulary • Kinds of Hotel Rooms

🎧 *Look at the pictures. Say the name of each kind of room.*

a single

a double

a suite

a smoking room

a nonsmoking room

a room with a king-size bed

a room with a balcony

a room with a view of the ocean

Pair Practice

Practice the conversation and vocabulary with a partner. Use your own words.

A: _____ Hotel. _____ speaking. How may I help you?

B: Do you have a _____ available on _____?

A: Smoking or nonsmoking?

B: _____.

A: Let me check. Yes, we do. Shall I hold it for you?

B: _____.

☑ **Now you know how to make a hotel reservation.**

(reinforces the real conditional)

You and your partner are planning a trip to Mount Henry, a city 700 miles from where you are now. You would like to stay there for one week.

Partner A, turn to page 146.
Partner B, turn to page 146.

 **Look at the round picture on page 109. With a partner, create a conversation for the two men. Make statements with *if*. Use your own words.**

Listening with a Purpose

Focus Attention

🎧 *Listen to the ads for three hotels and a motel. Write checks (✓) on this chart.*

	The Park South Hotel	The Inn at Echo Lake	Maple Tree Motel	The Grand Hotel
pool				
king-size beds				
free breakfast				
exercise room				
mountain bikes				
low prices				
quiet				
restaurant at hotel				
free coffee				
good location				

Improvise

Work in groups. One is a travel agent.
The others are:

Mr. Suzuki

Mrs. Hardy

Mr. and Mrs. Phelps

Ms. Lim

Mr. Suzuki wants to stay at a good hotel or motel with a lot of extras in the center of town. He is traveling alone.

Mrs. Hardy would like a reasonable place in the center of town. She's traveling with her husband and four children.

Mr. and Mrs. Phelps are rich and are traveling together. Price is not important to them.

Ms. Lim is a foreign student traveling with her roommate. She is looking for a reasonable hotel or motel in the country.

Use the chart in Listening with a Purpose. Tell the travel agent your needs. Agent, help your customers find the right hotels.

Look at the pictures on page 109. With a partner, make true and false statements. If your partner makes a false statement, disagree and correct your partner's statement. Use your own words.

Receptive Model

Reading

A Personal Letter

Before You Read: Have you ever had a bad experience when you were on a trip? What happened?

Read the letter. 🎧

January 15

Dear Jess,

Thanks for that wonderful tour of Yale. It has a beautiful campus, and we're so happy you're there.

Grandpa and I got to Miami two days ago. The weather here is wonderful—80 degrees and sunny. That's quite a change from back home. Unfortunately, the hotel our travel agent chose, the Yellow Bird Inn, was a disaster. Enclosed are some photos we took at the hotel. If I need a travel agent in the future, your Aunt Susan is the last person I will call. I should remember not to do business with relatives.

We expected three delicious gourmet meals a day. Instead, we got juice, burnt toast, and assorted jams for breakfast and peanut butter and jelly sandwiches for lunch. For dinner we got tough turkey with cold yams. Our dessert at both lunch and dinner was yellow Jello in the shape of a bird. Can you imagine?

We expected a beautiful room. Instead, our room was dirty, it faced a garbage dump, and the toilet didn't flush. When I called the front desk to complain, someone put me on hold for twenty minutes. You know Grandpa. He always says, "No use complaining." But this time Grandpa was so upset that he went downstairs to speak with the manager. The manager was so rude to him that Grandpa almost had a heart attack! That manager belongs in jail.

Anyway, we're packing our bags, and we're planning to stay with Sophie. If you want to reach us, we'll be at her place until February 16. Let us know how your classes are this term. What courses are you taking? How are your professors? Do you have time for your music?

We're enclosing a check. Buy something you really want. I bet you'll buy something for your computer. Please let us know what you get, and good luck this semester. And yes, we'll visit you again soon.

Love,
Grandma and Grandpa

Comprehension: Drawing Conclusions

*Mark the following statements **true** or **false**.*

	True	False
1. Jess is a student at Yale University.	☐	☐
2. The grandparents' home is probably in a cold climate.	☐	☐
3. The grandparents like peanut butter and jelly sandwiches.	☐	☐
4. The grandfather often complains.	☐	☐

Writing

A Thank-You Note

Pretend you are Jess. Answer the letter from your grandparents. Thank them for the money. Answer their questions about school and ask them a few questions.

Jesse Harris
Gray Hall
Yale University
New Haven, CT 06515

Mr. and Mrs. John Harris
c/o Mrs. Sophie Rons
6450 Collins Avenue, Apt. 305
Miami Beach, Florida 33141

Dear Grandma and Grandpa,

Thanks so much for the check.

Pronunciation

/dʒ/ and /y/

Underline the following words in the letter from Jess's grandparents on pages 104–105.

/dʒ/	/y/
jams	yams
jail	Yale
Jello	yellow
juice	use
Jess	yes

🎧 *Now listen and repeat.*

🎧 *Listen to these sentences. Repeat each one after the speaker.*

1. He's going to Yale.
He's going to jail.

2. I really like yellow.
I really like Jello.

3. What's the use?
What's the juice?

4. He said, "Yes."
He said, "Jess."

5. I bought some jams.
I bought some yams.

Now, with a partner, take turns reading the sentences one at a time, but not in order. Point to each sentence your partner reads.

How to **make a complaint**

Conversation

🎧 *Read and listen to the conversation.*

A: Front desk.

B: Hello. This is Patty Hardy in Room 302.

A: Yes, Ms. Hardy. What can I do for you?

B: Well, there aren't enough towels, and the air conditioner doesn't work.

A: Oh, I'm sorry. I'll take care of that right away.

B: Thank you.

🎧 *Listen again and practice.*

Vocabulary • In the Hotel Room

🎧 *Look at the pictures. Say the name of each thing.*

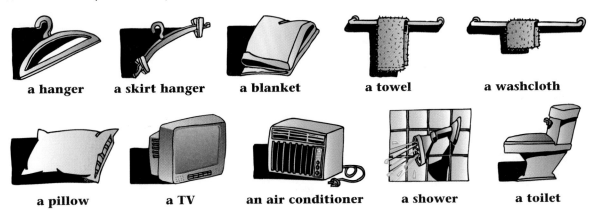

a hanger	a skirt hanger	a blanket	a towel	a washcloth

| a pillow | a TV | an air conditioner | a shower | a toilet |

Pair Practice

Practice the conversation and vocabulary with a partner. Use your own words.

A: Front desk.

B: Hello. This is _____ in room _____.

A: Yes, _____. What can I do for you?

B: _____.

A: Oh, I'm sorry. I'll take care of that right away.

B: _____.

☑ **Now you know how to make a complaint.**

HOW **TO** express preferences

Would Rather

Use **would rather** and a base form to talk about a preference.

> The weather is bad. I **would rather** wait until tomorrow to leave.

Would rather does not have **-s** in the third-person singular. It is not followed by **to.**

> He'**d rather** have lunch outside than inside.

To form the negative of **would rather,** place **not** after it.

> I'**d rather not** go out tonight.

To make questions with **would rather,** place **would** before the subject.

> **Would you rather** camp or stay in a motel tonight?

Grammar in a Context

*Complete the conversation with a form of **had better** or **would rather.** Use contractions if possible.*

Mrs. Hardy: Well, kids, _____ go to the beach or an amusement park?
                    1. you

Brad: Let's go to the beach.

Heather: You just want to see girls in bathing suits. It's too chilly for the beach.

Brad: Heather, _____ shut up!* You talk too much.
               2. you

Mr. Hardy: What about you, Teddy? Would you like to go to the beach?

Teddy: _____ go to an amusement park.
       3. I

Mr. Hardy: Maddie, what about you?

Maddie: I want to go to an amusement park, too. But Heather and I talked

about it. _____ go shopping first.
         4. We

Mr. Hardy: Well, whatever we do, _____ get going. We're wasting the day.
                5. we

***Shut up** is very rude. It is not used by Americans in polite conversation.**

Heart to **Heart**

I think...

In my opinion...   *because...*

I feel...

Talk with a partner. Compare your opinions.

What do you like about traveling? What are some problems you have had?

I don't think...

What about you?

Warm up: Talk about the pictures with a partner.
• What are the two men planning? • Ask your partner a question about the round picture. • Create a conversation for the two men in the round picture.

Then: Talk about the hotel room. Create a conversation for the man and the manager. OR Tell a story about the picture. Say as much as you can.

I can't stand filing!

Warm up: *Are some jobs more interesting than others?*
Read or listen.

Hi. Want to have lunch?

I sure do! I'm sick and tired of these files.

What's wrong? You seem down in the dumps.

Oh, I don't know. I guess I'm just bored.

Bored? With what?

With this job! There's no challenge. I can't stand filing. Using the copy machine isn't my idea of excitement.

And word processing is the most boring of all.

I just have to find something better.

Like what?

Well . . . Don't laugh. Like . . . flying.

Comprehension: **Understanding Meaning from Context**

Circle the choice closest in meaning to each sentence from the photo story.

1. I'm sick and tired of these files.

   a. I'm too tired to file.

   b. I don't like working on these files.

   c. I don't feel well.

2. You seem down in the dumps.

   a. You look like the garbage downstairs.

   b. You look very excited.

   c. You look unhappy.

3. I can't stand filing.

   a. I don't understand filing.

   b. I need to sit down when I'm filing.

   c. I hate filing.

4. I didn't realize you felt that way.

   a. I didn't make you feel that way.

   b. I didn't know you felt that way.

   c. I didn't feel that way.

HOW TO describe something you like or dislike/ greet a friend/promise to talk later

---

Gerunds

A gerund is a noun that comes from a verb.
Like a noun, it can be a subject or an object in a sentence.

gerund subject
Dancing is great.

gerund object
Alice loves ***cooking.***

Spell gerunds in the same way as present participles.

take → taking
swim → swimming
read → reading

TIP: Gerunds often follow verbs that express likes and dislikes: *love, like, enjoy, don't care (much) for, dislike, hate, can't stand.*

GRAMMAR TASK: Find gerunds in the photo story on pages 110-111. Be careful: don't confuse gerunds with present participles.

Grammar in a Context

Complete the conversation with gerunds, using the indicated words.

Melanie: So you really think you'd

enjoy _____ a pilot?
      1. be

Kathryn: Well, yes, I do. Like I was

saying, _____ in an
      2. work

office for the rest of my

life isn't exactly my idea

of an exciting career.

Melanie: But _____ is so different
      3. fly

from _____ in an office!
      4. work

What other things do you

like _____?
      5. do

Kathryn: Well, actually, besides _____ to fly a plane, I've always loved
6. want

_____ and anything to do with the theater. But _____ a living
7. act   8. earn

as an actor is really tough.

Melanie: Mmm-hmm. That's true.

Kathryn: I know it probably sounds silly, but _____ airplanes really has
9. fly

always been a dream of mine. I have an uncle who's a pilot, and he's always

going somewhere new. I love _____, and pilots can earn a lot of money.
10. travel

Melanie: You mean _____ a commercial pilot? You're really serious.
11. be

Kathryn: Yes, I am. I only have one life. I want to follow my dream.

Does that sound crazy to you?

Melanie: No, not at all. But it sounds really hard. It would mean _____
12. go

to flight school.

Kathryn: That really doesn't scare me.

Melanie: Well, how about _____ one of the airlines? I'm sure they can tell
13. call

you where to start.

Conversation

🎧 *Read and listen to the conversation.*

A: Hi, Jack. What's new?

B: Not much. Hey, I heard you have a new job.

A: Yes, I do.

B: How is it?

A: Pretty good.

B: Oh yeah? Well, how about getting together sometime? You can tell me all about it.

A: OK. I'll give you a call this weekend.

🎧 *Listen again and practice.*

Vocabulary • Words That Describe What You Like and Dislike

🎧 *Say the words and phrases.*

what you like	what you dislike	can be either
good	not so good	OK
pretty good	terrible	all right
great	awful	not bad
terrific	horrible	so-so
super	disgusting	
awesome		

Pair Practice

Practice the conversation and vocabulary with a partner.
Use your own words.

A: Hi, _____. What's new?

B: Not much. Hey, I heard you have a new _____.

A: Yes, I do.

B: _____.

A: _____.

B: _____. Well, how about getting together

sometime? You can tell me all about it.

A: OK. I'll give you a call _____.

☑ **Now you know another way to greet a friend, to describe something, and to promise to talk later.**

 **In Your Own Words** **Look at the last picture on page 121. With a partner, complete the conversation for Kathryn and the young man. Use your own words.**

Listening with a Purpose

Focus Attention 1

🎧 *Listen to the telephone conversation between Kathryn and Melanie.*

🎧 *Now listen again and make notes of Kathryn's likes and dislikes.*

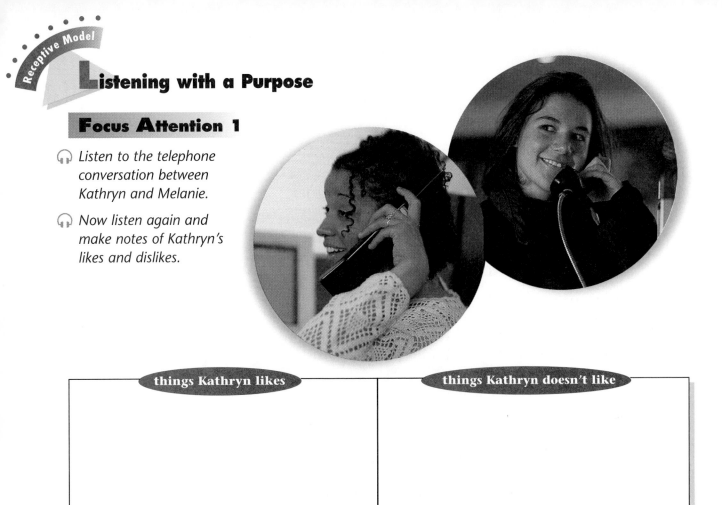

things Kathryn likes	things Kathryn doesn't like

Focus Attention 2

Read the following statements.

	True	False	I don't know.
1. In general, Kathryn likes flight school.	☐	☐	☐
2. Kathryn dislikes getting up early.	☐	☐	☐
3. Kathryn likes her roommate.	☐	☐	☐
4. Kathryn enjoys her classes.	☐	☐	☐
5. Kathryn likes the food at flight school.	☐	☐	☐
6. Kathryn loves flying.	☐	☐	☐
7. Kathryn likes her instructor.	☐	☐	☐
8. Kathryn is fond of New Orleans.	☐	☐	☐
9. Kathryn likes the weather in New Orleans.	☐	☐	☐

🎧 *Now listen again, and mark each statement **true, false,** or **I don't know.***

Reading
A Magazine Questionnaire

Before You Read: How well do you know yourself? Think about your likes and dislikes. Read the magazine article and questionnaire. 🎧

Psychology Tomorrow   **February**

Follow Your Dream
By Sally Russo

How do you feel about the choices you have made—in your career, in your studies, in your choice of friends, or even a spouse? Pleased? Satisfied? Disappointed? Research has shown the importance of following our dreams. The happiest people are the ones who take the time to know themselves, to understand what they enjoy doing.

This month's questionnaire is the first of three questionnaires designed to help you know yourself better. Next month we will follow up with a questionnaire about studies. And April's issue will include a questionnaire designed to help you evaluate the choices you have made in your social life.

Some people like working for others, being part of a big organization; others prefer being more independent, or self-employed. If you work in the office of a big company or if you are thinking of choosing an office career, this questionnaire will help you assess your satisfaction with your career choice, or suggest a more independent career.

*Read the following questions and check the choices that describe your likes
and dislikes. Then read about your score below.*

	1		**2**
☐	I like spending time with others.	OR	☐ I prefer working alone.
☐	I like dressing well for work.	OR	☐ I love working in old clothes.
☐	I prefer sharing decisions with others.	OR	☐ I like solving problems myself.
☐	I don't mind commuting.	OR	☐ I like working at home or near home.
☐	I like being part of a team.	OR	☐ I like making all the decisions myself.
☐	I don't mind having a boss.	OR	☐ I like being my own boss.
☐	I like meetings.	OR	☐ I hate meetings.
☐	I don't mind doing paperwork for others.	OR	☐ I dislike doing paperwork for others.

If you checked more than three boxes in the second column, you should think
twice before working in an office setting. We hope this helps you follow your
dream!

Comprehension: Drawing Conclusions

*Author Sally Russo has an idea of the kind of
person who likes working in an office.*

*Look at the questionnaire and try to describe
that person, according to Ms. Russo's ideas.*

 **Look at the first picture on page 121. With a partner, talk
about the women in the office. Make true and false statements
about the picture. Correct your partner's false statements. Use
your own words.**

Writing

A Description of Your Likes and Dislikes

Look again at the questionnaire in
Psychology Tomorrow *magazine.*
Use the results to write a paragraph
about what you like and dislike about
your job.

I like working with other people.

What's My Job?

(reinforces questions and answers)

Service Occupations

🎧 *Look at the pictures. Say the name of each occupation.*

a letter carrier   **a sanitation worker**   **a paramedic**   **a police officer**   **a firefighter**

One student chooses an occupation from the list above. The others ask the questions from the chart. Guess each other's occupations.

questions	answers	
	yes	**no**
1. Do you work outside?		
2. Is your job sometimes dangerous?		
3. Do you help people?		
4. Do you save lives?		
5. Do you need to be in good physical condition?		
6. Do you fight crime?		
7. Do you see the same people every day?		
8. Do you give things to people?		
9. Do you use a large truck?		
10. Do you use a lot of water in your work?		

 Write one more question.

_____

Pronunciation

Rising Intonation to Confirm Information

Listen to the following words and phrases that come from the photo story on pages 110–111. Do the speakers' voices rise or fall at the end of each one?

1. Bored?

2. Flying?

3. A flight attendant?

4. You?

5. A pilot?

6. OK?

Listen again and repeat.

TIP: Rising intonation has several meanings. It can indicate a question, or it can indicate that the speaker wants to check or confirm information. In both cases, the sentence is written with a question mark.

Now listen to the following sentences. Write a question mark for the ones with rising intonation.

1. They'll do it__

2. He's a nurse__

3. Happy__

4. Kathryn is a pilot__

5. They love working hard__

6. You'd like to be a flight attendant__

7. You will__

I think...

In my opinion...

because...

Go back to the questionnaire in the February issue of **Psychology Tomorrow**. Complete it for yourself. Then compare your responses with those of a partner. Where do you disagree? Tell your partner why you feel the way you do about your responses.

I feel...

I don't think...

What about you?

Improvise

Reread the photo story on pages 110–111, Grammar in a Context on pages 112–113, and the Conversation on page 113.

Look at these names of occupations.

More Occupations

a house painter

a waiter

a chef

a waitress

a mechanic

a receptionist	**a secretary**	**an engineer**	**a cashier**
an architect	**a manager**	**a banker**	**an actor**

Choose one of the occupations above. Then have a conversation with your partner. Ask and answer questions about what you like and what you dislike about your occupation and your new job. Use the photo story, Grammar in a Context, and the Conversation for ideas. But use your own words.

Warm up: Talk about the women in the first picture.
• What are their occupations? • Tell your partner everything you see in the picture. • Then talk about the other pictures.

Then: Create conversations for the women. Talk about their jobs. Are they happy? Do they like their work? Why or why not? Then tell a story. Say as much as you can.

We'll have to make a deposit right away.

Warm up: *Look at the pictures. What are Vic and Barbara talking about?*
Read or listen. 🎧

Hi, Barb. What are you doing?

Oh hi, Vic. . . . I'm balancing the checkbook—or trying to.

You know, honey, if we don't start saving some money, we won't be able to go to Cancún next spring.

Boy, I just can't figure this out. We're short $125.

Let's see, now. Did you write any checks you didn't tell me about?

Well, let me think. . . . Uh, yeah, I think I wrote a few.

Take a look in your checkbook. How many did you write? And how much were they for?

Oh no! Vic! Those checks are going to bounce! We'll have to make a deposit right away.

You're right. Give me the bank's number. I'll call and do an electronic transfer.

Uh . . . looks like three checks . . . for about . . . $300. Sorry. I forgot to tell you.

Comprehension: Understanding Meaning from Context

Circle the choice closer in meaning to each underlined phrase or sentence.

1. We're short $125.

    a. We have an extra $125.   **b.** We need $125 more.

2. If we don't start saving some money, we won't be able to go to Cancún next spring.

    a. putting some money in the bank   **b.** spending our extra money

3. Those checks are going to bounce!

    a. Those checks will go to the wrong bank.   **b.** We don't have enough money in the bank for the checks.

4. We'll have to make a deposit right away.

    a. write more checks   **b.** put money in the bank

5. I'll call and do an electronic transfer.

    a. We'll put money in the bank by telephone.   **b.** We'll change banks.

HOW TO **talk about future abilities and obligations/ ask someone for money**

Will Be Able To and Will Have To

The future of *can* is *will be able to*.

> We *won't be able to* go to Cancún next spring.
>
> *Will* I *be able to* get cash?

The future of *have to* is *will have to*.

> We *'ll have to* make a deposit today.

GRAMMAR TASK: Find and underline examples of *will be able to* and *will have to* in the photo story on pages 122-123.

Vocabulary • Money and Banking

Look at the pictures. Say each word or phrase.

cash

a check

a traveler's check

a coin

a bill

an ATM card

a savings account

a bank balance

a credit card

Grammar in a Context

*Complete the conversations with **will be able to** or **will have to** and the indicated verbs. Use contractions if possible.*

Conversation 1

Mary Pinto: I have good news and bad news.

The good news is that the

bank _____ you money.
            1. be able / lend

Vic: That's great, Mary. _____
                          2. we / be able / get

the full amount?

Barbara: Uh-oh. What's the bad news?

Mary: Well, I'm afraid we _____ you as much as you asked for.
                        3. not / be able / lend

Vic: Why not?

Mary: Well, you owe a lot on your credit cards. You _____ some of
                                                            4. have to / pay off

that debt first. If you can do that, we'll lend you what you asked for.

Conversation 2

Mary: OK, Tim. Your account's open, and here's your ATM card. _____ it
                        5. You / be able / use
starting tomorrow. And here are your traveler's checks. You just need to sign them on the top line. Where are you going on your trip?

Tim: Brazil. I'm in a summer exchange program. . . . Uh, _____ my
                                                                6. I / be able / use
ATM card if I need extra cash?

Mary: In some places, yes. But _____ an extra charge because you'll be
                                        7. you / have to / pay
out of the country.

☑ **Now you know how to talk about future abilities and obligations.**

Conversation

🎧 *Read and listen to the conversation.*

A: Want to have lunch?
B: Yeah, I'd love to. . . . Uh-oh. I don't have any cash on me. Could I borrow $20?
A: Sure.
B: I won't be able to pay you back till Friday. Is that OK?
A: No problem.

🎧 *Listen again and practice.*

Vocabulary • Social Activities

🎧 *Look at the pictures. Say each phrase.*

have coffee

go to a show

go out for dinner

go out for a drink

see a movie

go to a game

Pair Practice

Practice the conversation and vocabulary with a partner. Use your own words.

A: Want to _____?

B: Yeah, I'd love to. . . . Uh-oh. I don't have any cash on me. Could

   I borrow _____?

A: _____.

B: I won't be able to pay you back till _____. Is that OK?

A: _____.

☑ **Now you know how to ask someone to borrow money.**

In Your Own Words

Look at the second picture on page 133. Create a conversation for the two men. Use your own words.

Improvise

Your partner asks to borrow some money from you. You are not sure that you want to lend it. Improvise a conversation. Give a reason why you can't lend the money. Then change partners. This time you ask to borrow money and your partner agrees.

Example: Gee, I'm really sorry. I don't have any cash on me.
• • • • • •

 **Heart to Heart**

I think...   *In my opinion...*   *because...*

With a partner, discuss these questions. Compare your opinions.

Is it hard for you to lend (give) money to other people? If someone asks you for money, do you usually say yes?

Is it hard for you to borrow (ask for) money from other people?

I feel...   *I don't think...*   *What about you?*

Pronunciation
/v/ and /b/

🎧 *Read and listen to the following words.*

/v/		/b/	
vest		best	
very		berry	
saver		saber	
gave		Gabe	
vote		boat	

🎧 *Listen again and repeat.*

🎧 *Now listen again. Circle the words you hear.*

1. vest   best   **3.** saver   saber   **5.** vote   boat

2. very   berry   **4.** gave   Gabe

The Money Game

(reinforces questions and answers)

Play in groups of three: two players and a judge.

Use two coins as place markers. Take turns. Toss another coin to move. One side of the coin lets you move one space. The other side lets you move two.

If you land on a space with a question, answer the question. If your answer is correct, take another turn. Judge, the answers are on page 146.

1 START	2 You buy something and pay 18 marks. What country are you in?	3	4 What's the monetary unit of Spain?
8	7 How many pennies are there in a British pound?	6	5 How many dimes are there in a U.S. dollar?
9	10 How many centimes are there in a French franc?	11 You buy something and pay 900 yen. What country are you in?	12
16	15 What's the monetary unit of Russia?	14	13 Name three countries where the monetary unit is the peso.
17	18 You just made a trip from one country to another. You want to change won into yuan. What country did you come from?	19 You have all your zlotys in a savings account. What country are you in?	20
FINISH	23	22 Many years ago your parents traveled to this country and brought back some cruzeiros. You go to the same country, but now the monetary unit is the real. What country is it?	21 Name three countries where the monetary unit is the dollar.

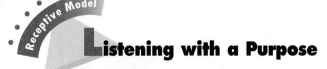
Listening with a Purpose

Determine Context

🎧 *Vic and Barbara are on vacation in Mexico.*
*Listen to this phone call. Mark the following statements **true** or **false**.*

		True	False
1.	The bank is calling Vic and Barbara.	☐	☐
2.	Vic and Barbara want to know today's date.	☐	☐
3.	Vic and Barbara want to speak to a representative.	☐	☐
4.	The information in the call is about money and credit.	☐	☐

Focus Attention

Look at the chart.

TODAY'S DATE
CHECKING ACCOUNT BALANCE
SAVINGS ACCOUNT BALANCE
CREDIT CARD BALANCE
AVAILABLE CREDIT

🎧 *Listen to the phone call again. Focus your attention on the numbers you hear.*
Fill in the information on the chart.

HOW **TO exchange currency**

Conversation

🎧 *Read and listen to the conversation.*

A: May I help you?

B: Yes. I'd like to change some traveler's checks into U.S. dollars.

A: All right. How much money would you like to change?

B: What's today's exchange rate?

A: Let's see. Oh. It's 7.9 today.

B: OK. I'll change $200, please.

A: Can I see your passport, please?

🎧 *Listen again and practice.*

Pair Practice

Practice the conversation with a partner. Use your own words.

A: May I help you?

B: Yes. I'd like to change some _____ into _____.

A: All right. How much money would you like to change?

B: What's today's exchange rate?

A: Let's see. Oh. It's _____ today.

B: OK. I'll change _____, please.

A: Can I see your passport, please?

☑ **Now you know how to exchange currency.**

Before You Read: What is money? What kinds of money do you use?
Read the article. 🎧

• Your Money •

Is Cash on the Way Out?

by Andrew Chen

People have used "money" for thousands of years. But what is money? When we think of money today, we most often think of cash: coins and paper bills. But this hasn't always been true. Humans have used (and still do use) other things to pay for goods and services, ranging from beads and other valuable things to bartering—trading goods and services for other goods and services.

Today, however, it looks like cash is starting to disappear. More and more, we're replacing cash with electronic money. We're using credit cards and ATM cards instead of coins and bills. The reason for this change is probably our global culture, our financial interdependence— from region to region and country to country. And it's so convenient to go shopping by telephone or by computer screen, buying things we've never seen from stores we've never visited. Distance is meaningless in cyberspace.

The movement away from cash to other kinds of money has its advantages and disadvantages. Traditional money is real. It's easy to pay with cash for a movie or for an ice-cream cone on the street. It's faster than writing a check or using a credit card. And the payment happens all at once—no bill will come later in the mail. The best thing of all, though, is that cash can't "bounce."

On the other hand, money is bulky. Coins are heavy and make holes in our pockets. Some people don't even like to handle money because it is dirty and covered with germs! But most of all, it's inconvenient for things that cost a lot. Imagine trying to buy a car with cash. How much easier it is to just take out a credit card or write a check.

Whether we like it or not, the trend is clear: We're going to see less and less cash in the future.

Comprehension: Understanding Meaning from Context

Circle the choice closer in meaning to each underlined word or phrase.

1. Humans have used (and still do use) other things to pay for goods and services, ranging from beads and other valuable things to <u>bartering</u>—trading goods and services for other goods and services.

    a. paying with money   **b.** exchanging items or services

2. On the other hand, money is <u>bulky</u>.

    a. big and hard to carry   **b.** small and easy to carry

3. Some people don't even like to <u>handle</u> money because it is dirty and covered with germs!

    a. touch   **b.** pay with

4. Whether we like it or not, the <u>trend</u> is clear.

    a. cash   **b.** direction

5. Distance is meaningless in <u>cyberspace</u>.

    a. computer communication   **b.** stores

Comprehension: Drawing Conclusions

Which of the following statements are true? Place a check mark next to those statements.

☐ **1.** Cash is a convenient method of payment if we want to buy a computer.

☐ **2.** In the past, regions were not so dependent on each other.

☐ **3.** Today it is impossible to buy things from stores that are far away.

☐ **4.** Sometimes cash is better than electronic money.

Writing

A Composition

Write a composition of two paragraphs about the advantages and disadvantages of credit cards. In the first paragraph, write about the advantages. In the second paragraph, write about the disadvantages. Use Chen's article for ideas and examples from your experience. Begin with a title.

Example:

The Advantages and Disadvantages of Credit Cards

Credit cards have made my life easier in many ways. First,

Warm up: Talk about this picture with a partner.
• Where are the men at 4:55? • What day of the week is it?
• Where do they go? • What happens there? • What do they want to see? • Where do they go after the movie?

Then: Create conversations for the men. OR Tell a story. Say as much as you can.

Review, SelfTest, and Extra Practice

Part 1

Review

Name That Food.

🎧 *Read or listen to the television quiz show **Name That Food.***

Marty: Good evening, ladies and gentlemen. I'm Marty Sousa, the host of *Name That Food*. Tonight we have with us Fred Hardy and Kathryn Nelson. Fred, could you please tell the audience a bit about yourself?

Fred: Sure, Marty. I'm Fred Hardy from Baltimore, Maryland. I'm a computer programmer, and I'm here tonight with my wife and four children. Do you mind? Hi Patty, Brad, Heather, Teddy, Maddie.

Marty: Great family. Tell us, Fred, what do you enjoy doing for fun?

Fred: I love traveling. My family and I have visited thirty-five of the fifty states in the United States, and we've been to Mexico and Canada, too.

Marty: That's wonderful, but isn't it expensive?

Fred: Well, we're fond of camping, so it's not too bad.

Marty: Kathryn, what about you?

Kathryn: My name is Kathryn Nelson, and I started flight school three months ago. I'm crazy about flying.

Marty: Oh. That's very interesting. I guess we're going to see more and more women pilots. Well now, it's time for our game. Remember, you will have three seconds to name that food. We'll begin with Fred. Ready?

Fred: Yes, Marty.

Marty: OK. Now listen carefully. If you order pie à la mode, what will you get on your pie?

Fred: Ice cream.

Marty: Right you are. You have one point. Kathryn, it's your turn. Are you ready?

Kathryn: I hope so.

Marty: OK. If you mix a peach and an apricot, what will you get?

Kathryn: A tangerine?

Marty: Gee, Kathryn, I'm sorry. The correct answer is a nectarine. Well, don't worry. This is just the beginning. But before we go on, we'll pause for a commercial.

a peach

an apricot

a tangerine

a nectarine

SelfTest

Comprehension: Confirming Content

*Read or listen to the quiz show again. Then mark the following statements **true, false,** or **I don't know.***

	True	False	I don't know.
1. Fred Hardy and his family have visited all fifty states in the United States.	☐	☐	☐
2. Fred Hardy likes camping.	☐	☐	☐
3. Fred Hardy wins the first point.	☐	☐	☐
4. *Name That Food* is on television every Tuesday night.	☐	☐	☐
5. If you order pie à la mode, you will get pie with cheese.	☐	☐	☐
6. If you mix an apricot and a peach, you will get a nectarine.	☐	☐	☐

Improvise

With two partners, improvise a quiz show on geography, history, or general knowledge. One person is the host/hostess, and the other two are contestants. The host/hostess introduces the show. Then the contestants tell about their jobs and what they enjoy doing in their free time. The host asks each contestant a question.

Part 2

Review

A Commercial

🎧 *Listen to the commercial.*

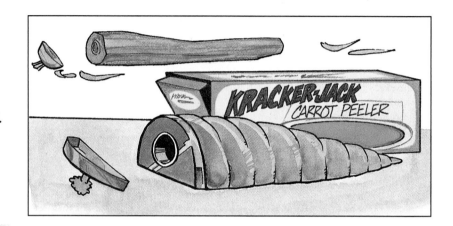

SelfTest

Grammar

Complete the text of the commercial by choosing the correct forms.

_____ you _____ the taste of freshly peeled carrots? Of
　　1. Don't / Aren't　　　　　　**2.** love / loving

course you _____. Who _____? But _____ you just
　　　　　3. are / do　　　　　**4.** don't / doesn't　　　　**5.** don't / aren't

_____ _____ carrots? Well, you're in luck.
6. hate / hating　　**7.** peel / peeling

If you _____ us $49.95, we _____ you our Kracker-Jack Carrot
　　　8. send / are sending　　　　　**9.** sent / 'll send

Peeler. It's fast and fun to use. If you _____ a carrot in the Kracker-Jack Carrot
　　　　　　　　　　　　　　10. put / will put

Peeler, two seconds later you _____ a perfectly peeled carrot. But you
　　　　　　　　　　11. 'll have / have had

_____ fast because this special offer is only good for the next six weeks. So, if
12. 'd better act / 'd rather act

you _____ eat carrots than peel them, send $49.95 right away to: Kracker-Jack
　　13. 'd rather / 'd better

Carrot Peeler, Box 2390, Hollywood, CA 90027.

Complete the sentences with the correct quantifier.

Ms. Jackie Cracker is the inventor of the Kracker-Jack Carrot Peeler. Jackie has invented

_____ other products, but none of them have made _____ money. At first, Jackie
1. several / much   **2.** much / many

had _____ trouble selling the Kracker-Jack Carrot Peeler, but after she began advertising
    3. some / any

on TV, _____ people began buying the peeler. With the money Jackie makes, she plans
       4. many / much

to buy _____ land and _____ horses. She also plans to save _____ money
     5. some / a few   **6.** a little / a few   **7.** some / any

to work on her next invention—a coffee cup warmer.

Writing

Write a commercial for some new kitchen product.
Use the commercial above as a model.

Checking In at the Maui Bilton

🎧 *Read or listen to the conversation.*

SelfTest

Comprehension: Factual Recall

🎧 *Read or listen to the conversation again. Complete the following statements.*

1. The Hardys have a _____ for a suite at the Maui Bilton.

2. Mrs. Hardy says there aren't enough _____.

3. The gym is on level _____.

4. Maddie wants to go to the _____.

5. It will _____ in half an hour.

Improvise

Work with two partners. Take turns. One of you works at the front desk of a hotel. The other is a bellhop, and the third is a hotel guest. The guest checks into the hotel and goes to the room. Have conversations. Use your own words and say as much as you can.

Extra Practice

Part 4

Review

Quiz Shows

Read the article about quiz shows.

Quiz Shows

Why are quiz shows so popular? According to a recent survey, people enjoy watching quiz shows for several reasons.

First, they like the challenge to contestants and the chance to test themselves. People also like learning something new in an easy way and without having to study. And finally, viewers enjoy seeing ordinary people—people like themselves—win a great deal of money in a short time. Some quiz shows require a lot of factual knowledge, while others require very little. However, all quiz shows include a bit of good luck.

Self**T**est

Comprehension: Understanding Main Ideas

Give three reasons why people like quiz shows.

1. _____

2. _____

3. _____

SOCIAL LANGUAGE SelfTest

Circle the appropriate statement or question to complete each of the following conversations.

1. A: _____

    B: No problem.

        a. Have you eaten here before?

        b. Could you please press eight?

        c. Here we are.

        d. Weren't you in this class last year?

2. A: Isn't this weather great?

    B: _____

        a. Yes, it is.

        b. You're right. It isn't.

        c. You're wrong. It is.

        d. No, it's great.

3. A: _____

    B: Sure. Right over there.

        a. Is there a library?

        b. Could you tell me where the library is?

        c. You'd better find us a library.

        d. Would you rather take us to the library?

4. A: How much time do we have left?

    B: _____

        a. By four o'clock.

        b. You're on time.

        c. A few minutes.

        d. In the afternoon.

5. A: Would you like me to check the oil?

   B: _____

    a. Please.

    b. Be glad to.

    c. Don't worry.

    d. I like it.

6. A: Can you believe this weather?

   B: _____

    a. You'd rather.

    b. You'd better.

    c. It's really awful.

    d. Here it is.

7. A: I'm leaving right now.

   B: _____

    a. Aren't you leaving?

    b. You are?

    c. You'd rather not.

    d. When are you leaving?

8. A: I'm going to the bank. Does it close at six?

   B: _____

    a. Yes. It's 5:45. Hurry. You'd better not make it.

    b. You'd better go to the bank.

    c. Yes. It's 5:45. Hurry or you won't be able to make it.

    d. Yes, I'd rather go to the bank.

9. A: When can I see Dr. Smith?

   B: _____

    a. Of course.

    b. Sure. No problem.

    c. You'd better see a doctor.

    d. He won't be able to see you before next Monday.

10. A: _____

   B: You'd better see a doctor.

      a. I feel terrible.

      b. Dr. Smith is a better doctor than Dr. Klein.

      c. Have you tried chicken soup?

      d. May I help you?

11. A: _____

   B: Now.

      a. Will you study?

      b Would you rather study now or later?

      c. Do you study English?

      d. How long do you want to study?

12. A: How may I help you?

   B: _____

      a. I'd like to make a reservation for Monday the twelfth.

      b. By car.

      c. I'd rather make a reservation for Monday the twelfth.

      d. Yes, you may.

13. A: How's your new job?

   B: _____

      a. So what?

      b. So tell me about it.

      c. So-so.

      d. Do you have a new job?

14. A: _____

   B: No problem.

      a. I won't be able to pay you back until I get to the bank.

      b. What's new?

      c. Oh yeah?

      d. I adore flying.

Activity Links

Unit 2

Info-Gap
A Visitor from the Year 3001
Partner B

Your Answers

1. Yes / will.
2. No / won't.
3. No / won't.
4. Yes / will.
5. Yes / will.

Partner A is a time traveler from the year 3001. Partner B, use the cues below to ask Partner A questions 6–10 about year 3001.

Your Cues

6. pandas / be / extinct?
7. people / have / robots in their houses?
8. there / be / solar-powered houses?
9. there / be / a world government?
10. people / live / in Antarctica?

Bonus Question: What's your opinion of the answers to these questions?

Unit 3

Grammar with a Partner answers for pages 33–34.

1. Venus / the hottest
2. I / the most common *or* the commonest
3. Australia / the smallest
4. whale / the heaviest
5. Chicago's O'Hare / the busiest
6. Mercury / the fastest
7. The / the most common *or* the commonest
8. The Himalayas / the highest
9. The South China Sea / the largest
10. giraffe / the tallest

Unit 4

Improvise
Patient:

Choose an ailment or an injury. Answer the receptionist's questions. Fill in the form on page 45. Then see the doctor.

Here are some useful expressions:

I feel awful / terrible.

I have a terrible _____.

I have a pain in my _____.

I hurt my _____.

I was skating when . . .

I think I broke my _____.

I've had _____ for _____.

Doctor:

Look at the information on each patient's form. Ask the patient questions about that information. Then ask your patient about the problem. Make a suggestion.

Here are some useful expressions:

How can I help you?

How long have you had this problem?

Have you taken anything for it?

Have you done anything for it?

Have you tried _____?

You need to go to the hospital.

Try _____.

Call me _____.

Unit 5

Info-Gap
Olympic Mania

Partner A asks questions. Partners B, C, and D give answers. For each question, two partners will give the correct information. One partner will give an incorrect answer.

Partner B	Partner C	Partner D
1. Rome	Greece	Greece
2. Since 1892.	Since 1896.	Since 1896.
3. The U.S.A.	The U.S.A.	China
4. Boxing	Football	Boxing
5. Cross-country skiing	Cross-country skiing	Baseball
6. The Soviet Union and China	The Soviet Union and the U.S.A.	The Soviet Union and China
7. Romania	Bulgaria	Romania
8. 197	197	302

Unit 6

Info-Gap
Watch Your Pronunciation!

Partner B: You want to know where the following places are:

the library
the bank
the stationery store

Example:

A: Excuse me. Could you tell me where the nearest _____ is?

B: Yes. It's on the corner of _____ and _____.

OR

Yes. It's on _____ between _____ and _____.

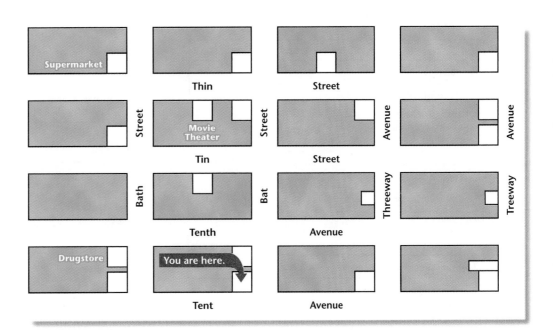

Info-Gap

Partner A, your partner has information about the Planeview Hotel and the Central Hotel.

Get information about the two hotels from your partner. Write it on the chart. Then answer Partner B's questions.

Finally, discuss the reasons for staying at each hotel and some reasons to go by car, by train, or by plane.

Examples:

Information

A: How much will it cost if we stay at the Planeview Hotel?

B: Forty-five dollars.

Discussion

A: If we stay at the Central Hotel, we'll be in the center of town.

B: Yes, but it'll cost fifty dollars more a night.

Hotels

	Planeview Hotel	Central Hotel
Rates		
Meals included?		
Other information (location, types of rooms, etc.)		

Travel

	Car Rental	Train	Plane
Cost	$200.00 / week plus gas	$180.00	$250.00
Travel Time	10 hours	7 hours	1 1/2 hours

Partner B, your partner has information about the cost and time it takes to travel to Mount Henry.

Get the information from your partner. Write it in the chart. Then answer Partner A's questions.

Finally, discuss the reasons to go by car, by train, or by plane, and the reasons to stay at each hotel.

Examples:

Information

A: How much will it cost if we rent a car?

B: If we rent a car, it'll cost $200.

Discussion

A: If we rent a car, it'll take much longer.

B: That's true, but we'll have a car the whole time.

Hotels

	Planeview Hotel	Central Hotel
Rates	$45.00 per night	$95.00 per night
Meals included?	no meals	breakfast included
Other information	$10.00 transportation to town by bus 30-minute bus ride to town 20 minutes to town by taxi or car We will hear airplanes landing and taking off because the hotel is near the airport.	Central location $10.00 parking fee

Travel

	Car Rental	Train	Plane
Cost			
Travel Time			

Unit 10

The Money Game answers for page 128.

2. Germany
4. peseta
5. 10 dimes
7. 100 pennies
10. 100 centimes
11. Japan
13. Mexico, Chile Colombia
15. ruble
18. Korea
19. Poland
21. Australia, Canada, United States
22. Brazil

Appendices

Key Vocabulary

This list represents key words and expressions presented in Book 2. Book 2 also includes vocabulary that was presented in Book 1. The definite or indefinite article is included to help students with usage.

Unit 1

Nouns

a romance
a relationship

Verbs

argue
have to (for future)
reach
remember
ring
shall
sleep
wonder

Social activities

go to the beach

have coffee
have dinner
see a movie
study together

Adjective

right (correct)

Expressions

Expressions of location

behind me
in front of me
near me
next to me

Greetings and responses

Glad to see you.

Great to see you.
How are you doing?
How are you?
How's it going?
Nice to see you again.
Nice to see you, too.

Ways to accept an invitation

I'd love to.
Sounds good to me.
Sure.
That's fine.

Present and future time expressions

next weekend
this afternoon

this weekend
today
tomorrow
tonight

Other expressions

How'd you like to...?
Maybe some other time?
That's too bad.
Would you like to...?
See you later.
Actually...
Fine.
OK.
Great.

Unit 2

Nouns

Fruits

a banana
a grape
a kiwi
a lemon
a lime
a mango
a melon
a pear
an apple
an orange

Vegetables

a carrot
a pepper
a potato
a tomato
an onion
celery
corn
garlic
lettuce
spinach
squash

Other nouns

a dentist
a favor

Verbs

Everyday favors we do for others

drive (a person) to (a place)
mail some letters
buy some groceries
take some clothes to the cleaner
wait for a delivery

Other verbs

rain
return
visit

Expressions

Be glad to.
What's up?

Other

There will be...
will / won't

Unit 3

Nouns

Clothing materials

cotton
denim
fur
leather
nylon
wool

Other nouns

boots
a jacket
a moment

a salesperson
a window

Verbs

check
exchange
fit
mean

Adjectives

Clothing sizes

extra large
large
medium

petite
regular
small

Other adjectives

busy
cheap
colorful
common
easy
expensive
far
fast
healthy
heavy
high

hot
long
tall
big
loose
short
small
tight
useful

Expressions

Excuse me.
How much...?
Just a minute.

Unit 4

Nouns

Ailments

a cold
a cough
a fever
a headache
a rash
a sore throat
a stomachache
a toothache
the flu

Remedies

a heating pad
a hot shower
a hot water bottle
a pain killer
chicken soup
ice
tea with milk and
     honey

Other nouns

doctor
patient
receptionist

Verbs

hope
spend
try

Adjectives

awful
horrible
not great
sick
so-so
terrible

Adverb

absolutely

Prepositions

for
since

Expressions

Gee, that's too bad.
How long...?
I'm really sorry to hear
     that.
I'm so sorry to hear
     that.
Oh, no.
What's the matter?
What's wrong?

Unit 5

Nouns

Personal items

a briefcase
a checkbook
a purse
a wallet
keys

pills
(sun)glasses

*Places and things in the
house*

a bathroom
a closet
a desk
a medicine cabinet
a refrigerator

Other nouns

advice
matter
pocket
suggestion

Verbs

complain
could

hate
look for
quit
should
support

Adjective

crazy

Unit 6

Nouns

Family relationships

an aunt
an uncle
a cousin
a sister-in-law

a brother-in-law
a father-in-law
a mother-in-law
in-laws

Other nouns

an elevator
the weather
a floor

Verb

hold

Adjectives

To describe the weather

beautiful
great

fantastic
gorgeous
unbelievable

Expressions

By the way...
Why don't you...?

Unit 7

Nouns

On the highway

a pickup truck
a police car
a station wagon
a tow truck
a traffic jam
a truck
a van
an accident
an ambulance

Other nouns

a driver
a gas guage

a jack
a road
a seat
a seat belt
a speed limit sign
a speedometer
a steering wheel
a tire
gasoline
oil
services
a windshield
yards *(for measurement)*

Verbs

At the gas station

check (the oil, tires)
wash (the windshield)

Other verbs

fill up
had better
slow down

Adjectives

At the gas station

medium
premium
regular

Other adjectives

back
flat
front
spare

Adverb

ahead

Quantifiers

a few
a little
a lot of
any
many
much
several
some

Expressions

Sure thing.
would rather

Unit 8

Nouns

Kinds of hotel rooms

a double
a nonsmoking room
a room with a balcony
a room with a king-
    size bed
a room with a view of
    the ocean
a single

a smoking room
a suite

In the hotel room

a blanket
a hanger
a pillow
a shower
a skirt hanger
a toilet
a TV
a washcloth

an air conditioner
a towel

Other nouns

a hotel
a motel
the front desk

Verbs

take care of
work *(The _____
    doesn't work.)*

Adjectives

available
enough

Adverb

right away

Expression

What can I do for
    you?

Unit 9

Nouns

Occupations

an actor
an architect
a banker
a cashier
a chef
a firefighter
a house painter
a letter carrier
a manager
a paramedic
a police officer

a receptionist
a sanitation worker
a waiter
a waitress

Other nouns

a job
cooking
dancing
swimming
taking

Verbs

act
can't stand

dislike
don't *care* (much) for
earn
fly
get together
give _____ a call
hate

Adjectives

*Words and expressions
that describe what you
like and dislike*

all right
awesome

disgusting
not bad
not so good
OK
pretty good
so-so
super
terrific

Expression

What's new?

Unit 10

Nouns

a bank balance
a check
a checking account
a coin
a credit card
a deposit
a savings account
a bill

a traveler's check
an ATM card
cash
credit
dollars
the exchange rate
a passport

Verbs

Social activities

go out for a drink

go out for dinner
go to a game
go to a show
have lunch

Other verbs

borrow
bounce (a check)
change (money)
lend
pay
pay (someone) back
pay off

Expressions

Want to (do
something)?
will be able to
will have to

Common Irregular Verbs

Base Form	Simple Past	Past Participle
be	was, were	been
beat	beat	beaten
become	became	become
begin	began	begun
bend	bent	bent
bet	bet	bet
bite	bit	bitten
blow	blew	blown
break	broke	broken
bring	brought	brought
build	built	built
buy	bought	bought
can	could	been able to
catch	caught	caught
choose	chose	chosen
come	came	come
cost	cost	cost
cut	cut	cut
dig	dug	dug
do	did	done
draw	drew	drawn
drink	drank	drunk
drive	drove	driven
eat	ate	eaten
fall	fell	fallen
feed	fed	fed
feel	felt	felt
fight	fought	fought
fit	fit, fitted	fit, fitted
fly	flew	flown
forget	forgot	forgotten
freeze	froze	frozen
get	got	gotten
give	gave	given
go	went	gone
grow	grew	grown
hang	hung, hanged	hung, hanged
have	had	had
hear	heard	heard
hide	hid	hidden
hit	hit	hit
hold	held	held
hurt	hurt	hurt
keep	kept	kept
know	knew	known
lead	led	led
leave	left	left
lend	lent	lent

Base Form	Simple Past	Past Participle
let	let	let
light	lit, lighted	lit, lighted
lose	lost	lose
make	made	made
mean	meant	meant
meet	met	met
must	had to	had to
put	put	put
quit	quit	quit
read	read	read
ride	rode	ridden
ring	rang	rung
rise	rose	risen
run	ran	run
say	said	said
see	saw	seen
sell	sold	sold
send	sent	sent
set	set	set
sing	sang	sung
shake	shook	shaken
shoot	shot	shot
show	showed	shown
shrink	shrank	shrunk
shut	shut	shut
sit	sat	sat
sleep	slept	slept
slide	slid	slid
speak	spoke	spoken
spend	spent	spent
spread	spread	spread
stand	stood	stood
steal	stole	stolen
stick	stuck	stuck
sweep	swept	swept
swim	swam	swum
swing	swung	swung
take	took	taken
teach	taught	taught
tear	tore	torn
tell	told	told
think	thought	thought
throw	threw	thrown
understand	understood	understood
wake	woke, waked	woken, waked
wear	wore	worn
win	won	won
wind	wound	wound
write	wrote	written

Spelling Rules for Participles and Gerunds

Add -*ing* to the base form of the verb.

> read + -ing = reading

If the verb ends in silent -*e,* drop the -*e* and add -*ing.*

> take + -ing = taking

If the verb ends in a single vowel and a single consonant, double the consonant and add -*ing.*

> run + -ing = running

But don't double the final consonant if the verb end in *w, x,* or *y.*

> fix + -ing = fixing

If a verb has two or more syllables and ends in a single consonant, double the consonant and add -*ing* if the last syllable is stressed.

> permít + -ing = permitting
> lábor + -ing = laboring

If a verb ends in -*ie,* change the -*ie* to *y.* Then add -*ing.*

> die + -ing = dying